PENGUIN BOOKS

CHARACTER PARTS

John Mortimer is a playwright, a novelist and a former practising barrister. During the war he worked with the Crown
Film Unit and published a number of novels before turning
to the theatre with such plays as *The Dock Brief*, *The Wrong
Side of the Park* and *A Voyage Round My Father*. He has
written many film scripts, radio plays and television plays,
including six plays on the life of Shakespeare, the Rumpole
plays, which won him the British Academy Writer of the
Year Award, and the adaptation of Evelyn Waugh's *Brideshead Revisited*. His translations of Feydeau have been
performed at the National Theatre and are published in
Penguin as *Three Boulevard Farces*. Penguin publish his
collections of stories *Rumpole of the Bailey*, *The Trials of
Rumpole*, *Rumpole's Return*, *Rumpole for the Defence*,
Rumpole and the Golden Thread and *Rumpole's Last Case* as
well as *The First Rumpole Omnibus*. Two volumes of John
Mortimer's plays, his acclaimed autobiography, *Clinging to
the Wreckage*, which won the *Yorkshire Post* Book of the Year
Award, *In Character*, a series of interviews with some of the
most prominent men and women of our time, *Charade*, his
first novel, and *Paradise Postponed*, which was dramatized on
television, are also published by Penguin. John Mortimer
lives with his wife and their two daughters in what was once
his father's house in the Chilterns.

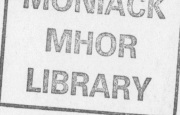

Character Parts

JOHN MORTIMER

PENGUIN BOOKS

Penguin Books Ltd, 27 Wrights Lane, London w8 5tz (Publishing and Editorial)
and Harmondsworth, Middlesex, England (Distribution and Warehouse)
Viking Penguin Inc., 40 West 23rd Street, New York, New York 10010, USA
Penguin Books Australia Ltd, Ringwood, Victoria, Australia
Penguin Books Canada Ltd, 2801 John Street, Markham, Ontario, Canada L3R 1B4
Penguin Books (NZ) Ltd, 182–190 Wairau Road, Auckland 10, New Zealand

First published by Viking 1986
Published in Penguin Books 1987

Made and printed in Great Britain by
Hazell Watson & Viney Limited,
Member of the BPCC Group,
Aylesbury, Bucks
Typeset in Plantin

All but one of these interviews appeared in the *Sunday Times* and are dedicated to Don Berry, in memory of life before Wapping.

Acknowledgement is gratefully made by the author and publishers for:

Extracts from *Sweeney Todd* by Stephen Sondheim, copyright ©
Revelation Music Publishing Corp., 1979. Reproduced by kind
permission of Warner Bros Music Ltd.

Lines from 'Meditations in Time of Civil War' by W. B. Yeats.
Reproduced by kind permission of A. P. Watt Ltd on behalf of Michael
B. Yeats and Macmillan London Ltd.

Extract from *Live Flesh* by Ruth Rendell, copyright © Ruth Rendell,
1985. Reproduced by kind permission of A. D. Peters & Co. Ltd on
behalf of Century Hutchinson.

Contents

Contents

Bollocks to the Bench of Bishops

LORD HAILSHAM

'Why do you think you were passed over as leader of the Conservative Party when Macmillan retired? Why didn't you ever become Prime Minister?'

'The truth is that I was a victim of my own success. I was best known as Party Chairman at the time. I had to do things the leader can't do. I did the bell and bum-bags. All that sort of thing.'

They were stirring times in 1963. The nerve of the Conservative Party had been badly shaken by the Profumo affair. Harold Macmillan was unwell and had privately chosen Lord Hailsham as his successor. Hailsham had earned a good deal of publicity by ringing a bell with wild abandon at a Party conference and appearing in a pair of bathing trunks on Blackpool beach in order to plunge into a rough sea in October. This rash act, which he now referred to as the affair of the 'bum-bags', gave the impression, the ex-Chairman said, 'of physical vigour, a certain amount of hardihood and a capacity to be unafraid of ridicule, all of which I suppose was quite genuine'. He disclaimed his hereditary Viscountcy, became plain Mr Quintin Hogg and his hat was in the ring.

Twenty-two years later Quintin Hogg, now once again Lord Hailsham, Baron Hailsham of St Marylebone, Lord High Chancellor of England, sat in his cavernous room in the House of Lords and played thoughtfully with a pile of paper clips on his blotter. On a table in the corner his full-bottomed wig and his great black, three-cornered hat awaited their ceremonial uses.

'I was the advocate for the Party and I put my case extremely high. I made enemies, of course. I was accused of being vulgar, and they were perfectly right. I was vulgar. They judged me to be less good than Alec Douglas-Home!' Lord Hailsham looked up then; he was shaking with one of his fits of delighted laughter, his stout, 78-year-old body surmounted by the impish, uncombed head of a moderately outrageous schoolboy. 'That was the worst judgement the Conservative Party ever made.'

'But there was no election for leader. It was all done by word of mouth?'

'Word of mouth. Yes. All sorts of strange things were happening. Ted Heath went up to Scotland and for the first time in his life he *shot a stag*! Can you imagine that?' Lord Hailsham was laughing again. 'I think Ted Heath was Warwick the Kingmaker.'

'Was it all a great disappointment to you?'

'Not at all! I was just not selected. It must have been much worse for Ted Heath. To be chosen and then de-stooled. In the presence of the tribe! To be de-*stooled*.' His lips pursed in a long and hilarious double 'o'. 'What a terrible humiliation!

'Besides which I've known all the recent Prime Ministers and not one of them died happy in his bed. Except Macmillan. Yes. I think he'll die quite happy.'

'Is Macmillan a wonderful actor in the House of Lords?'

'Of course. The old boy's a superb performer. But when he was Prime Minister he was always rather *piano*. Rather quiet and understated. And you know why? The best of his generation was killed in the 1914 war. And he could see their ghosts all looking down at him from an imaginary gallery, all saying, "Look down there. It's little Harold! They've made him Prime Minister, and we were *cleverer* than him." That made Macmillan rather quiet.'

'So it didn't have any permanent effect on you. Not being Prime Minister, I mean?'

'Only one thing. I used to write poetry regularly. And when I was passed over I suddenly found that I couldn't write a line.'

*

'Of course I got on very well with my father as you did with yours. You and I were both born into the law.'

'What would your father have said if he'd known you would eventually become Lord Chancellor, as he was?' I asked Lord Hailsham.

'My father! He'd have thought it was absolutely impossible. He died in 1950, so sadly he never saw me take silk. But if he'd known that I was going to be Lord Chancellor, and for longer than him, and *twice*! Well, I tell you, he'd have laughed like a drain!'

'In your book *The Door wherein I Went* you seem to be so certain in your faith in Christianity and the British legal system and the Conservative Party. I mean, you were very loyal to your father and the possibility of any other outlook doesn't seem to occur to you. But if you'd been born the son of a Brahmin, or a highly respectable Socialist agnostic?'

'Then I'd probably have been a Socialist. One's convictions grow out of the seed and soil one's born in.' Lord Hailsham made an admission which I tried to pursue. 'So if we had both been born the sons of successful South London bank robbers . . .?' I began to ask. 'I really can't tell you what I'd've been like if I'd had a drunken father and a promiscuous mother,' the Lord Chancellor interrupted me, 'I can't tell you that at all!'

'You also wrote, when you started in politics, that you didn't agree with Socialist remedies, but you accepted many of the premises of your Labour contemporaries. You said the one characteristic of your political beliefs was your hatred of unemployment and poverty. That was in the 1930s.'

'That's perfectly true.'

'So don't you find it rather dispiriting that under this Government we seem to be back to the bad old days of mass unemployment?'

'The only thing I know about economic rules' – the Lord Chancellor had his head down now and was making a neat pile of paper clips – 'is that there *are* no economic rules. Unemployment's not so bad now anyway, because of the Welfare State. I'll tell you one thing. It'll be a lot better in a few years' time. There'll be a lot more jobs to go round because there'll be a lot less people of employable age, although they'll have an enormous number of old people to look after.' His head came up laughing again. 'I'll be dead by then, of course.

'When I was in charge of the North-East I did create some jobs. I went for growth objects, like building frigates or a bridge over a motorway with British steel. But I must admit that if some dear old clergyman said save this dear old pit for the sake of this dear old village I didn't take much notice.'

'When you were at the bar you used to lose your temper in court?'

'I always worked on a quick flash-point, yes. I don't think it won me many cases.'

The organization of the legal profession, much loved by most barristers including Lord Hailsham, can be criticized as forming a closed shop with as many restrictive practices as in those old-fashioned trades unions lawyers denounce. What did the Lord Chancellor think of those who wanted to change the system?

'Most people who want to reform it are grossly ignorant of the way it works, and so ignorant that they don't even realize how ignorant they are. It will evolve gradually. When I started, barristers were charging special fees to go to Quarter Sessions they didn't belong to, or to go off their circuits. That's stopped, and so has the "two counsel" rule under which a QC has to be employed with another barrister. Of course, if someone wants to indulge in a case which lasts eighty-seven days they need two barristers. That's entirely their own look-out.'

'Why's litigation so ridiculously expensive? You're all right if you happen to be a huge corporation or if you're on Legal Aid, but for the ordinary litigant it's impossible.'

'The middle of the road man who gets run down in the middle

of the road? They've got a system of litigation insurance in West Germany. We're looking into that.'

'How do you appoint a Judge?'

The Lord Chancellor, who rules over a vast department of some ten thousand court officers and staff, appoints all Judges, QCs and magistrates, sits as a Judge himself in the House of Lords appellate committee and presides over debates from the Woolsack. It is a great deal of power for a Government appointee and member of the Cabinet, and in the early years of this century was abused by the appointment of political friends as Judges.

'I tell you. I have files on all the barristers, awful files with all the gossip, everything in them, including their drinking habits.' I looked nervously round the room, trying to work out which drawer contained the bulging dossier proving my own entire unsuitability for high judicial office. 'Then I consider what Division of the court I have to appoint a man to, Queen's Bench, Chancery or the Family Division. I ask the Judge who's Head of that Division for his opinion. If it's a veto I usually take it. If he recommends someone I have to consider the personality of the Head of the Division. Is he a volatile sort of fellow who'd have favourites? Being a Judge means a drop in income for successful barristers, but I get very few refusals. It needs a good deal of experience to tell what's going to happen to a good advocate when he gets on to the bench. He may start losing his temper, or be like Dick Crossman's father and find it impossible to make up his mind about anything. Or he may suffer from a bad case of "Judgeitis".'

'What's "Judgeitis"?'

'Put briefly, pomposity and self-regard.'

'What do you think of prisons?'

'Ghastly! Fortunately I've never had to sentence anyone to gaol. The punishment's meant to be depriving people of their liberty, not squeezing them in three to a cell and making them slop out. All that sort of thing. It's appalling.'

'What's the answer?'

'Build more prisons, of course.' The Lord Chancellor was studying his paper clips intently, faced with a stain on our society which no Government is going to win votes by removing.

'And the death penalty?'

'In principle I'm in favour. There's a great temptation to a man who does a rape or a violent crime to bump off the only witness. *But*, and it's a huge *but*, let me say this. It's tolerable to have the death penalty. It's tolerable *not* to have the death penalty. What's *in*tolerable is to keep chopping and changing about it. And now we've had a free vote in the House of Commons I don't think we should change. If it's going to be reintroduced it's got to be reintroduced for keeps.'

'Do you find sitting on the Woolsack in the House of Lords very boring?'

'Intensely. You're not like the Speaker of the House of Commons. You've got no control at all over the debates, so I sit there as little as possible. Gerald Gardiner, that great ass-scetic, sat there hour after hour like a stuffed owl. When I'm sitting I amuse myself by saying "Bollocks!" *sotto voce* to the Bishops.'

'Don't you think the Bishops are entitled to speak out if they think the Government's behaving immorally?'

'They totally misunderstand their role. The Church was told to be the leaven in the lump, the salt in the dish. It wasn't meant to make all people think in the same way. Don't they understand that the Holy Spirit directs some people to be Socialists and some to be Conservatives? The Bishops treat everyone like patient peasants waiting to be told which way to vote.'

'Do you think there'll be some sort of eternal judgement on you after your death?' The idea of the Almighty as a sort of celestial Lord Chief Justice was one which, having been abandoned by the Bishops, seems to persist among lawyers who can no doubt understand the conception.

'I'm sure that there'll be a general judgement day. And I'll have to face judgement in my own particular case. Ooh yes, the auditors will catch up on me! I only hope I'll have the sense to plead guilty and throw myself on the mercy of the court. I know that I have done wrongs.'

'What sort of wrongs?'

'Oh, private matters. Entirely private matters,' the Chancellor said quietly and studied his pile of paper clips.

'What do you do when you're not being Lord Chancellor?'

'I used to walk in the Alps before my legs gave out. I still read Greek. I've re-read the whole of the *Odyssey* in the last few years.' Quintin Hogg got a First at Oxford and used to sit next to Enoch Powell, when they were in Opposition, swapping Greek quotations. He has translated Catullus and said that writing poetry should come as naturally to a man as singing in his bath.

'What else do you read?'

'Biographies. There's a good new book on Thomas More' – the Chancellor mentioned one of his distinguished predecessors – 'and Patrick Devlin's book on the trial of Dr Bodkin Adams, alleged to have poisoned his patients. It's the only book I know written by a Judge about a case he tried. That was the only trial in which I knew the Judge *and* prosecuting counsel *and* the defendant *extremely* well.'

'You knew Dr Bodkin Adams?'

'Ooh yes I did. Oooh yes!'

'Do you think he was guilty?'

'I wouldn't care to say what I think . . .' And Lord Hailsham was laughing again. 'But he must have had quite a lot of explaining to do to the recording angel. The auditors would have been after him, ooh yes!' There was a moment's silence while I pondered on Lord Hailsham's friendship with an Eastbourne Doctor accused of murdering his old lady patients.

'Are you depressed by the state of Britain?'

'Yes. By the loss of religious faith. I recognize that we had a century of triumph between 1815 and 1914. Our decline since then has been a painful spiritual experience to the thinking patriot. But

I believe that we're still part of a living tradition which began when the Athenians won the Battle of Marathon.'

'And are you happy?'

'I would have to say I've never been happy since my wife died seven years ago.' Lady Hailsham was killed tragically in a riding accident in Australia. 'But I'm eternally grateful to Margaret for giving me this job. Work's a great therapy. If you're working you can hold your head up high, not engage in wretched fits of crying, things like that. Yes, I'm grateful to Margaret for giving me the job, and the miracle is she hasn't asked me to go.'

'So you're not going?'

'Not while I'm fit to carry on.'

'And what was your happiest time?'

'When the children were growing up and I was at the bar. Then I was happy.'

'But you've written no more poetry since you missed becoming Prime Minister?'

'That's not *quite* right. I've written three poems very recently. All of them are religious.'

Bewigged and gowned, preceded by his mace bearer, his purse bearer, who carries the magnificently embroidered bag which used to hold the Great Seal of England, and followed by his train bearer, the Lord Chancellor in procession is an impressive figure. There is a story that once, processing through the corridors of Westminster, Lord Hailsham spotted a friend and called out his Christian name 'Neil!', whereupon a number of American tourists fell to their knees in reverence. At the moment he has no intention of joining the powerless ranks of ex-Lord Chancellors. The great offices of state are clearly there to be relished, and to be used, as the Chancellor happily mutters 'Bollocks!' to the bench of Bishops, as some distraction from private grief.

Boyle's Law

JIMMY BOYLE

'I'm thirty-eight now. Since I was twelve years old, you know how much freedom I've had in the whole of my life? I mean counting approved school, Borstal and all that sort of thing?'

'No, tell me.'

'Twelve and half months.' Jimmy Boyle smiled, as though he also found the fact unbelievable. He had been out for about five months, since he finished his fifteen-year sentence for a Glasgow gangland murder, and was sitting on the settee in his Victorian house in Edinburgh. It was the sort of room, with its red-painted ceiling and big white ball of a paper lampshade, with the boxed Beethoven symphonies round the hi-fi and his own remarkable sculptures echoing Epstein and Giacometti, that might be inhabited by a comfortably off *Guardian* reader in NW1.

Sarah Boyle, the pretty psychiatrist daughter of the former film censor John Trevelyan, brought in breakfast. They had married when Jimmy Boyle was in prison. We had hot croissants and black coffee, cheese with herbs in it, and grapes and tangerines, and Mr Boyle talked with the released urgency of a man who has spent five and a half years of his life in solitary.

During breakfast I tried to remember that Jimmy Boyle had fought his way down to the lowest and most brutal depths of the penal system. He had been kept in a cage measuring 3ft by 11 where he had lain naked, smeared with his own excrement, in the

17

vain hope, he said, of keeping the warders from beating him up with their batons and kicking him with their large, polished boots.

He had, on his own account, wounded three fellow prisoners. I looked round the room again for signs of this extraordinary past; all I could see was a sculpture of a small silvery figure crouched among tall black posts, and a long white scar on the side of Jimmy Boyle's neck.

'My father was a safe-blower. He had a lot of respect in the community. He died when I was very young.'

'The community was the Gorbals,' I said. 'Is that why you decided to become a "hard man" around the age of eight?'

'Well, it seemed obvious. As kids we'd hang around the chippie and the chip man would kick our arses for us, and tell us to get out of it. Then Big Ned, the hard man of the street, would come along and get a load of fish and chips and say, "Come in, boys, I'll treat you" – and he wasn't even paying. So we learnt who got the respect.

'It was usual in our street to have your big brother to protect you, but my eldest brother was a fashion designer, a homosexual, and the next one had an accident when an iron railing fell and broke his skull, so neither of them could fight. I had to do the battles for all us boys. My Ma got a job cleaning out the trams when my father died. She was always worried about us getting into trouble. She was a Catholic. We all were. I used to go to confession and tell about my thieving to the priest and I felt a lot better for it.'

'You weren't a mugger really, just a petty thief?'

'That's right. We thieved from shops, silly things, bottles of bleach, bars of soap. We did it for the excitement and to show we had quick hands. But, you know, there were no Fagins. There were always good-living people ready to buy the bleach off us, or the bottles of cheap whisky we thieved at Christmas.'

'The violence came in fights with other gangs of children?'

'That's right. My gang was called the Skull.'

'When did you first feel the attraction of violence?'

'Once when a kid was chasing me and I was frightened. I stopped and lofted up a brick and he ran away. I wasn't frightened any more. I suppose I had a feeling of power.

'The grown-ups never stopped us fighting. They used to enjoy watching us kids do battle in the cinema queue to get into the sixpenny seats. At school, the masters used to point to us in assembly and say, "You'll end up in Barlinnie Prison." They always said it as though we were rather remarkable, as though they were proud of us. It made you feel good.'

'The community you lived in didn't entirely disapprove of crime?'

'Of course not. You were always supported by your family, against the system. And when you got into prison you felt you were the victim – the incident that got you there was in the past. Now you were suffering the injustice.'

'What sort of injustice, if you'd committed the offence?'

'It was Governors. I never knew a Governor who didn't tell me, "If my officer said he didn't hit you then I'm going to believe my officer." One even said, "If my officer swears he saw you racing round the prison yard on a red motor bike then, as far as I'm concerned, my officer's telling the truth." '

'What made you decide to fight prison all the time? I mean, you upset desks on Governors and . . .'

'I was hard on Governors, yes. You see, I'd been tried for murder twice, the first time for capital murder when I was eighteen, and I was acquitted twice. When I was tried for killing Babs Rooney I knew they were out to get me.

'The jury came back with a verdict and I told myself not to show any emotion. There was a little court usher and when they said "Guilty" he raised his two thumbs in a victory sign to the police. I said to myself to hell with him, I'm not going to let that little usher beat me. A year later, when I was starting my fifteen-year-minimum sentence, I was going to try to commit suicide with a razor blade, but the thought of how pleased that usher would be stopped me just in time.'

'Is that what kept you going in five and a half years' solitary confinement?'

'It's a funny thing about solitary. You think you'd want to see people. Not at all. I dreaded the door opening. I just wanted to be left alone.'

'Could you read?'

'They gave you a book a week. You'd divide it up into seven, a bit for each day. It's funny how you always kept a page or two extra for a real splash-out on Saturday night. You couldn't choose the book, the screw just gave you the next one off the trolley. By a bit of luck I got *Crime and Punishment*.

'I think that when I was in solitary I found another person inside myself. I realized I'd got it all wrong, but I still couldn't bring myself to come out of the cage and say, "Peace, brother!" And I never thought I'd ever be let out. Not ever.

'You know I didn't kill Babs Rooney? Babs was someone I'd met in prison and once or twice on the outside. We quarrelled that night and I cut him. I know who actually did the murder and we tried to cover up for him because he was a friend of mine. Sometimes in solitary I'd say, "Oh, Babs, I wish I'd really killed you!" I decided not to protest about the verdict. Pat Meehan was in the next cell and he was obsessed because he had been wrongly convicted. He used to think he was fitted up by the Russians, or MI5, and we used to say, "Shut up, Pat. You were fitted up by the police like everyone else." It destroyed him. So I decided to accept the verdict and fight the system.'

While Jimmy Boyle was doing press-ups and reading Dostoevsky in solitary confinement, a remarkable experiment took place in the Scottish penal system. A Special Unit was created where a few long-term prisoners might live in humane conditions and, to some extent, run their own affairs in prison meetings. Four of the men already in the Special Unit suggested that Jimmy Boyle might be allowed to join them. The cage was opened and, to his initial terror and dismay, Mr Boyle was no longer treated as an animal.

'This warder called Ken Murray was opening a lot of parcels in the Special Unit, and he suddenly handed me a pair of scissors and said, "Come along, help me."

'That did something to me. I couldn't imagine a screw trusting me with a weapon. Anyway I helped him and he said, "We're all in the dark here. We've got to try to make this place work."

'At first we went around whispering together. We thought all our talk was being bugged. The screws didn't wear uniform. They wore white coats and we thought they'd got us into some sort of hospital and they were trying to prove us crazy. I was always terrified of being certified, when you'd really be in the world of no hope.

'It took two years for me to get to trust the Special Unit, and I was there for about eight altogether.'

During this time Jimmy Boyle started to produce sculpture, which was exhibited in Edinburgh, and wrote his book *A Sense of Freedom*. He also got married. The prison authorities, perhaps displeased because he had sent a copy of his manuscript out to an aunt who got it published while he was still in custody, sent Jimmy Boyle back to serve the last two years of his sentence in a conventional prison. He was released after doing every day of his recommended fifteen years.

At a quarter to nine that morning Jimmy Boyle had met me at Edinburgh airport. He is a compact, broad-shouldered, good-looking man with a soft Scottish accent (his gangland nickname was Baby Face), who had been up at six and out jogging.

'You can't explain crime just by having been born in the Gorbals,' I said over breakfast.

'I think you can. Sarah and I are going to start a centre to help teenagers from deprived areas. Part of the money from my new book's going into that, and I've set up a trust to help children in Glasgow. They need some help. With the despair of unemployment, they're on heroin now, a lot of them. They've only got one thought, to get enough money each day to buy smack.'

He drank coffee and looked up at the red ceiling. 'All the murderers I knew in prison, none of them killed anyone deliberately.'

'But there must be some deliberate criminals. You knew the Krays. How did you get on with them?'

'I think the Krays were highly respected round the East End of London. People there thought they'd done very well. It's the culture, you see.'

I wondered, for a moment, why all reformed criminals start to talk like sociologists writing for *New Society*. Then I asked, 'Don't you think there are some people who have to be locked up?'

'I suppose Brady's one, the Moors murderer. I don't think he'd be safe with the public.'

'Your gang used to be unlicensed money-lenders, charging 25 per cent interest a week. That sounds a rather mean sort of crime.'

'People needed us. If they didn't pay us they might get bashed on the nose. If they didn't pay the legitimate guys they got all their furniture taken, that was much worse for them.'

'Are you convinced prison does no good?'

'It creates crime. Old lags used to leave and say to the screws, "Hold my snout, I'll be back on Monday." You can get anything in prison – knives, drugs, anything you want. Prison is an entirely criminal society.'

'How's Jimmy?', said the taxi driver who drove me back to the airport. 'How's his marriage going?' No doubt, in our strange society, Jimmy Boyle is a sort of star to the young people he is genuinely trying to help, as he was to the children of the Skull gang and even to the screws who beat him up.

No doubt he has committed appalling acts of violence, and his explanations for that part of his life may be inadequate. Crime can't be written off as being just the accident of environment or birth. Perhaps there is something to be said for the Christian doctrine of original sin; but, if you believe in that, you must also accept the possibility of redemption. Jimmy Boyle's story does show what a creative penal system might do for the whole of our society in reforming criminals. Meanwhile there may still be men who are spending tonight in a cage, in the final reduction of our custodial system to an obscene absurdity.

The Giddy Joke of It

THE BISHOP OF DURHAM

'I am not alarmed. I know very well that no ecclesiastical process could possibly establish I'm a heretic.' And then the Bishop smiled. 'They appointed me because I was well known as a particularly *orthodox* theologian. And that's the giddy joke of it!'

Auckland Castle, home of the Bishops of Durham, Princes Palatine since the twelfth century, seemed an appropriate place to be discussing heresy on a May afternoon. The sun was burnishing the grey stone walls of the Scotland wing, where the warlike Bishops of Durham used to keep their Scottish prisoners and which now accommodates a lady who carries on a small business clipping pet dogs. It warmed the huge kitchen garden, encouraging the vegetable seeds, and it fell on the pink, smiling face of Dr David Jenkins, who has achieved the strange feat of making the Church of England headline news. 'Why,' he said in one of his frequent bursts of happiness, 'they're even talking about God in the cake shop!'

The man who is now England's fourth senior Bishop, an automatic member of the House of Lords, who occupies the castle where the old banqueting hall has been turned into the largest private chapel in Europe, grew up in Catford in a family of Methodists. 'My father was an insurance inspector for the Scottish Providence Society. My grandfather had been a master carpenter and a lay preacher. My mother was a rather upstage Wesleyan. My father was a more down-market "Primitive".'

'At the age of twelve you were converted to Anglicanism?' I had imagined the streets South-East of London as the road to Damascus and the small, talkative Grammar School boy turning, in a flash of blinding light, from the evils of Methodism to the true path of the C of E. The truth was apparently less dramatic. 'I came into contact with the Crusaders, a sort of evangelical Church of England society. They had a great deal to do with missions to China, that sort of thing.'

'How did they convert you?'

'Let's say, at Methodist Sunday School I was treated as though I was about eight years old. The Crusaders treated me as a reasonable, grown-up person. I'm not sure if that was it.' He sounded a little doubtful.

'Who influenced you most, your mother or your father?'

'That's a difficult one! Very difficult.' The Bishop is short, white-haired and extremely neat. Sitting in an armchair he thought with his entire body. When momentarily flummoxed he would throw his small, brightly shod feet into the air and lie almost prone in silent thought. When the words came pouring out, as they often did, he sat forward eagerly, his fingers ticking off points against each other. Now he looked vague, as though his past life didn't greatly interest him, and said, 'You know, I'm not awfully good at remembering.'

'Did you always believe in God?'

'Oh yes.' He was sure about that.

'And what did you want to be? Not an insurance inspector?'

'I always knew I'd be some sort of missionary. That was quite clear to me. Oh, and I read everything I could put my hands on. So I was sure to be an academic. I got a History scholarship to Oxford but then of course the war was on.'

'You were in the Royal Artillery. Do you think you actually killed anyone?'

'Oh no. I was very lucky about that. I got my commission on VE Day. And then I was sent to India. I suppose I was a Troop

Commander in India. Yes.' The Bishop looked back into his past as though at a country he seldom visited. 'I must have been a Troop Commander. How very odd!'

'But you weren't a pacifist.'

'Let's say, pacifism wasn't one of the things I thought about.'

After the war Dr Jenkins studied Theology for five years at Oxford, where he got a First and a fellowship at Queen's. After a spell with the World Council of Churches in Geneva he became Professor of Theology at Leeds. There seemed no one better qualified, therefore, to answer the questions which have long troubled me.

'What is God?'

There was a silence. The Bishop's legs shot out, his fingertips met, he searched for elusive words. Could it be that the question was as troubling to him as it was to me?

'I think . . . Yes!' The words seemed to hover in the air and he swooped on them. 'He is the power behind all things. He is present in all things. He is the promise of all things.'

'Is He a personal God?'

'Not *ultra* personalized.' The Bishop looked anxiously at his highly polished shoes and suddenly became more cheerful. 'I got into trouble recently for calling God "He, She or It".'

'Is "He, She or It" omnipotent?'

The Bishop blinked unhappily at the word. 'Let's say, there are no limits to His power.' From then on the 'She' and 'It' dropped quietly from the conversation. 'He can't be stopped. I know He can do anything that makes for worth.'

'Then what about the gas chambers? Could He have been stopped if He wanted to prevent the massacre of seven million Jews?'

'Oh yes . . . *that*.' He sat crouched now, rubbing his hand across his eyes as though suddenly exhausted. 'I'm afraid there's no simple answer, no guarantee that He'll stop this or start the other.

The whole thing is full of risk and uncertainty, for God and for us!' The idea of risk and uncertainty seemed to have rejuvenated Dr Jenkins; he was sitting forward eagerly, counting the words out on his fingers. 'God take risks on us and we have to take risks on God!'

'What are we risking? Is it like Pascal's idea of faith as a gamble?'

'Well, not quite such a cliché as Pascal.' He smiled tolerantly at me, as a professional actor might when discussing an amateur's shot at Hamlet in the village hall. 'But yes, we take the risk that belief may not only be nonsense but *bloody* nonsense. That's why I'm able both to believe passionately and to be quite agnostic at the same time.' The Bishop sat back in his chair, as though exhausted again by this considerable feat.

'If a belief in Christianity produces good results – I mean, if it makes people kinder, more compassionate, more concerned about the poor – does it matter if it's true or not?'

'That's either the 64,000-dollar question' – the Bishop sat up again somewhat startled – 'or a complete nonsense! No. The good is really true, and the most worthwhile thing is the discovery of the truth. St Augustine would have understood that.'

At a quarter to five, as instructed, the Bishop's daughter Rebecca, who acts as his secretary, came in with a tea tray which she put on the floor beside him. I sat quietly for a moment, conscious of not being St Augustine, and the Bishop said, 'It's quite fun, isn't it, talking like this?'

'About the Resurrection . . .'

Refreshed by his tea Dr Jenkins was game to tackle the Resurrection.

'I've been reading *Who Moved the Stone?* by Frank Morrison . . .'

'That's exactly the wrong approach! It regards the New Testament books as providing undoubted historical evidence which leads logically to a supernatural conclusion! Our curse is that we live in a scientific age and we can't believe that anything is real unless it has physical reality. Saint Paul wouldn't have any of our trouble, he'd have understood emotional truth and not been tied down to scientific facts.'

'But suppose I were a Judge sitting on a case which turned on the facts of the empty tomb. Suppose I'd heard all the witnesses, Mary Magdalene and her friends and the eleven disciples, everyone concerned. What would the correct verdict be?'

'The verdict would be "Not Proven".' It was, perhaps, an easy middle way which an earlier Bishop of Durham might have heard about from one of his Scottish prisoners.

'But would I find that the witnesses were telling the truth, or lying, perhaps to try and establish the miraculous claims of the Christian religion?'

'You would decide that they really believed what they were saying.'

'But most witnesses manage to convince themselves they're telling the truth by the time they get to court. Very few of them lie consciously.'

'I don't mean that they'd convinced themselves.' The Bishop became vehement. 'I mean that the evidence was true to them.'

I spent a moment trying to grasp the distinction which was no doubt clearer to a theologian than to a lawyer and then tried another line of cross-examination.

'If God is unstoppable, as you said . . .'

'Yes?'

'Then He *could* have arranged a miraculous resurrection of the body and the release from the tomb if He'd wanted to?'

'Oh yes.'

'By miraculous means?'

'Yes.'

'Then if He *could* have done it, does it really matter if He did it in this case or not? I mean, it only seems important to argue against the miracle of the Resurrection if you are using that to deny the existence of God . . .'

'No!' The Bishop was sitting upright again, his fingers ticking off arguments with great rapidity. 'Although He *could* have done it, it doesn't seem to be the way He goes about things. But the real point is that concentrating on the miraculous sidetracks people. It encourages them to believe in all sorts of other things like' – Dr Jenkins gave a small but visible shiver of disgust – 'spiritual healing! And then miraculous claims put ordinary, sensible people off Christianity. They say, "Tell that to the marines," and so they miss a great opportunity for good.'

'Do you believe Christ was God? Or a demi-God?'

'He certainly wasn't a demi-God. That would be heresy.'

'The Arian heresy?'

'Yes. This isn't easy to say.' There was a sudden silence. Outside the sun shone on the big, empty garden; the Bishop was again recumbent. Then he sat up, thoroughly awake. 'The man Christ is God!' he said. 'The reality which is Jesus is a man. That particular man is God being a man.'

I thought of the almost silent towns we had driven through, of Shildon with its torn-up railway lines and abandoned repair works, and wondered how immediately comprehensible the Bishop's thoughts would be to the average laid-off worker in the Locomotive Arms.

'The Bishop of London,' I warned Dr Jenkins, 'thinks you're a bit of a gnostic.' I have to admit that I knew no more of the gnostic heresy than could be gained by a brief visit to the *Encyclopaedia Britannica*. Apparently it formed the basis of a sect which flourished in the second century AD and its adherents believed they could attain salvation through superior and mystic knowledge which was inaccessible to the common people. The word seems now to be a mild term of abuse used by Bishops. 'How much of all this theology is really important to ordinary, suffering humanity?'

'It's vital! I have three great concerns, theology, spirituality and society, and they're all connected. The point is that theology tells you that God is what makes for worth and goodness. That's my answer to people who say Bishops shouldn't get involved in politics.'

'People like what's-his-name? – John Selwyn Gummer?' I mentioned, for what it was worth, the then Chairman of the Conservative Party, a man who thought Bishops should not meddle in matters best left to the Conservative Party.

'Mr Gummer!' The Bishop smiled. 'I think *he's* a bit of a gnostic, as a matter of fact.'

I thought of the way John Selwyn Gummer piped up on the wireless to announce that election defeats are really substantial victories. Perhaps this was due to his mystical knowledge unshared with the common people.

'Are you a Socialist?'

'My father was an Asquithian Liberal. I always took the Conservative side in school debates. I was against theoretical political beliefs. I always have been.'

'Your great hero, Archbishop William Temple, was a Socialist?'

'I suppose so. Along the lines of George Lansbury and Sir Stafford Cripps.'

'But you do involve yourself in politics, though after your consecration you said you were going to lie low like Brer Rabbit.'

'That was misinterpreted. I only meant that I was going away for the weekend.'

'But soon after that you hit the headlines by calling Ian MacGregor, the Chairman of the Coal Board, an elderly imported American.'

'The statement was entirely factual.' The Bishop seemed not in the least contrite. 'Nothing wrong with being old but he was completely out of touch. And appointing an imported American showed that Mrs Thatcher had no wish to reach a compromise with the miners. She was just out to pick a quarrel.'

'What did you think of Dr Runcie apologizing to Mr MacGregor for you saying that?'

'I think the Archbishop of Canterbury is in a very difficult position. He has to have daily dealings with the political powers that be.'

In a divided country it seems that nothing but good can come of Bishops preaching the virtues of compassion and reconciliation. Besides which there is little new under the sun; in the year 1882 Bishop Westcott called the disputing parties to the Palace at Bishop Auckland and settled a coal strike.

'How do you think you got made a Bishop?'

'We pass from the Great Mysteries to a small mystery. Since Mr Callaghan's time they instituted the Crown Appointments Commission. The Archbishop of Canterbury chaired the meeting which selected me. They chose two names to send up to the Prime Minister. Of course, you never know whose the other name was, or if you're the first or second choice. Traditionally Durham goes to a theologian and, as I say, I was *not* known as a liberal academic. My books have all been quite orthodox.'

The fame, some would say the notoriety, of Dr Jenkins arose from one television broadcast ('It's a witness to the enormous power of telly,' he said.) He appeared on a London Weekend programme called *Credo* on 29 April 1984. 'What I said was just clearing the ground really, the sort of thing we're doing today.' Dr Jenkins's words on *Credo* appeared to cast doubts on conventional beliefs in the Resurrection and the Virgin Birth. These views may have seemed old hat in the theological college but they deeply shocked the newspapers. However, of thirty-one Bishops polled, ten found Dr Jenkins's thoughts on the Virgin Birth acceptable, fifteen didn't disagree with him on the subject of miracles and nineteen were in favour of accepting Christians who denied Christ's divinity.

Whatever the Bishops may have thought, petitions were organized against Dr Jenkins's consecration; his wife and family received anonymous threats of death or attack; and the Reverend David

Holloway of Jesmond said it was like appointing a civil servant to the Ministry of Defence who had announced his intention of giving away the secrets of Cruise missiles. The Reverend John Mowll, vicar of an evangelical church at Buglawton, read out a protest in a loud voice at the consecration ceremony and was finally frog-marched out of York Minster. According to some people God made his views felt by striking that ancient building with lightning. However most responsible Christians might think that although God undoubtedly has the power to perform that dramatic act, actually doing so would not be quite his style.

'What's the worst sort of religion?'

'The worst sort? Oh, that's easy. Muslim fundamentalism. Jewish fundamentalism. The Christian "Moral Majority" in America. Having a bad religion's much worse than having no religion. You know, atheism once did a useful service in driving out bad religions.' And here Dr Jenkins gave one of his slightly impish smiles which must be the despair of his opponents. 'My worry is that perhaps we need another dose of atheism.'

'Do you think a lot about death? Your own death, I mean.'

'Well, I'm sixty. I've got to the age when it's become clear to me that I shan't go on for ever.'

'Do you believe in immortality?'

'I think I shall go on enjoying.'

'What do you enjoy? Do you read a lot?'

'Not as much as I should. There's all this administration.' He waved hopelessly at the yard-high stacks of files on his desk. 'Actually I'm quite good at that. I was a Staff Officer during the war. But I read Maigret in French. That really gives the smell of Paris. And I enjoy books about hunting.'

'Hunting?' For a moment I had an improbable vision of a small, pink-coated theologian pelting after foxes across the highest fences in County Durham.

'Tiger-hunting in India. There's a book by Jim Corbett called

Man-Eaters of Kumaon. I enjoy that very much. And then I go on Hellenic cruises and lecture. I'm just back from Thessaly and Mistra, the wonderful monastery on the mountain. But music is my great pleasure: Verdi's *Falstaff* and Mozart. You know what Karl Barth the German theologian said?' I had to confess that my chosen subject for *Mastermind* would never be the works of Karl Barth.

'He said, "If Mozart's not in Heaven I'm not going to stay there." I once told that to a very serious theologian and he said he couldn't agree: "Bach perhaps, but not Mozart." ' The Bishop laughed. 'Are you happy?' I asked. 'Oh yes. I'm usually happy.'

'I suppose death wouldn't be so bad if you could go on enjoying Mozart.'

'I expect to go on enjoying the sparkle of things. That's what's important. Religion's no good if it hasn't got sparkle.'

'Do you believe in Hell?'

'I think perhaps there's a way we can cut ourselves off from going on enjoying.'

'Enjoying is salvation?'

'Oh yes.'

'Is it available to people of other religions? Good Hindus . . .'

'Christ is the great example. But if you're a Hindu and lead that life as well as possible . . . Yes, I think so . . .'

'Or good atheists?'

'I would hope the goodness of atheists would eventually lead them to God.'

We were both silent, the questions were over. Dr Jenkins joined his hands together, resting before a Confirmation service and another round of talks and meetings; a good, usually happy man bubbling over with thoughts about great issues, not yet quite at home in a palace with seventy-five rooms and one cleaning lady who comes in the mornings. He is a man who, whatever they think of his views, has brought a bit of sparkle back into the Church of England.

'I sometimes wish I could be a Christian,' I heard myself say.

'Like many people you're probably on our wavelength. The difference between us is only paper thin. It doesn't do to fudge what divides us, but it's only as thick as a cigarette paper.'

I wondered, though, if Dr Jenkins was right about the attraction of miracles. Do those who embrace the faith like to think they need to do no more than penetrate a cigarette paper, do they long for a great leap in the dark?

It Could Have Happened
to Any Good-looking Girl

CHRISTINE KEELER

'Who was Christine Keeler?' A blank look came over the face of the intelligent, twenty-year-old girl in the office, and no flicker of recognition greeted the mention of Mr Profumo or Captain Ivanov, Stephen Ward or Mandy Rice-Davis, Peter Rachman or the Man in the Mask. These people have become lost in the past and are as unmemorable to the young as Campbell-Bannerman or Titus Oates, Sir Charles Dilke or Eleanor of Aquitaine. And yet, in their small way, the participants in the stirring, tragic and sometimes hilarious events of the 1960s contributed to history. After the full facts were known, after the rumours concerning a sexual orgy attended by eight High Court Judges had died away ('Two, conceivably, but eight – I just can't believe it,' Harold Macmillan is said to have murmured to a colleague), English public life had undergone a small change for the better. It was no longer possible to take those who seek to govern us entirely seriously.

In remembrance of old scandals, and those ever more extravagant headlines which added such a zest to the British breakfast table twenty-three years ago, I travelled to the World's End, or that part of it which lies at the bottom end of the King's Road, and then trusted myself to a vandalized, graffiti-stained lift. The flat on a high floor had fine views, little furniture, Christine Keeler's son's school reports (excellent) pinned on the wall and a picture of a knight in shining armour liberating a bound and scantily clad nymph from a tree – an article of faith, perhaps, as knights in shining armour have been noticeably absent in Miss Keeler's life. And there she was, forty-two years old and fussing with her cats, a woman who had been particularly beautiful. Time has struck Miss Keeler some moderately unkind blows, but she still walks like a model and her voice is ever soft, gentle and low, which King Lear thought an excellent thing in women. It's a voice which must have brought great comfort to the men who sought her company. I took Miss Keeler to lunch and no one in the restaurant seemed to recognize her. The puritans among them may have been glad to know that the wages of sin, if not death, are a tower block flat up a vandalized lift and a life on Social Security.

It was when we were tucking into the *nouvelle cuisine* (a curse which has come upon the world since Christine Keeler's heyday) that I asked her if she regretted her past of sensation and scandal. Was it, perhaps, something that made her feel different and more important than the anonymous teenagers of the early sixties? 'That's an easy one. I regret it terribly. It's been a tough life, but it's something that could have happened to anybody. Any good-looking young girl.'

The life that might, apparently, have happened to anybody started in a converted railway carriage in Wraysbury, Berks, a dwelling without a bathroom and, for most of Christine Keeler's childhood, without electricity. There she lived with her mother, a devout Catholic who 'sat in the room and saw God looking at her' and a step-father with whom she never got on.

'I left home when I was fifteen or sixteen to go and live with a girlfriend in Slough. She was pregnant. The landlord there jumped on me and we decided to move to a house in St John's Wood with two reps we'd met in the factory where we worked. We stole a car to get to London. I knew how to start it by putting a bit of silver paper in the ignition. It was just naughtiness really. I'd stopped believing in God when I was thirteen and another girlfriend of mine had died. When I got to St John's Wood I went to a Greek shop round the corner to get milk and a loaf of bread, and I got to know some people who ran a Greek restaurant. It was there I met a woman who introduced me to Murray's Cabaret Club.'

Mr Percival Murray ran an institution which sounds rather like Roedean. There was a head girl and strict rules. 'No bruises and you had to wear gold or silver shoes and have a hairdo every week. I was a showgirl. You got £8.50p a week and £5 for sitting with a customer. You got extra points if he bought more drink or a flower for you. The girls who got most points were sent down to sit out first. Of course, if you went home with them you might get £25 but that was nothing to do with the Club. I only went home with the ones I fancied. I always liked boys. There were a lot of boys around Wraysbury. All I wanted was fun. Nothing serious. To me life was for having a good time. I had a regular Greek boyfriend. I met Mandy Rice-Davis at Murray's. She was a bit of a bird-brain, but she was fun to be with. She'd come down from Birmingham and I'd come from Slough.'

It was at Murray's in 1959, when Christine Keeler was seventeen, that the most important meeting of her life occurred. She was 'sitting out' with an Arab called Ahmed, who always asked for her, and they were joined by Stephen Ward who was, by profession, an osteopath. Mr Ward asked for Christine Keeler's telephone number and she didn't write it down but said it quickly, half hoping that he would forget it. No such luck. Stephen Ward remembered the number well and actually visited the family in the railway carriage where he behaved, as always, like a perfect gentleman. Had Stephen Ward not been at Murray's that night he might still be alive; Mr Profumo, who knows, might be be Prime Minister and Miss Keeler might have lived as anonymously as any other young lady who sat out with gentlemen at Murray's Cabaret Club.

'I moved into Stephen's flat in Bayswater. No. I never had an affair with Stephen. I loved him but I didn't fancy him. We had two single beds and pushed them together. He made a bit of an approach, of course, but when he found out I wasn't keen he didn't go on with it. He really was a gentleman; I trusted him. Then I left Stephen for a while to live with Peter Rachman.'

'The landlord with an unconventional way of collecting rent. Did you fancy *him*?'

'Oh yes. He had a realistic attitude to human foibles. He simply couldn't understand why the man who I lived with wasn't keeping me. After a while I went back to Stephen. That's when I met Ivanov.'

And did she, I wondered, fancy Captain Eugene Ivanov, Naval Attaché at the Russian Embassy?

'He was more handsome than most of Stephen's friends. But he was a bit of a bore really, very serious and Red and always telling us how wonderful Russia was and grumbling all the time about England.'

When we met, Miss Keeler had told me she didn't drink at lunchtime because 'it turns me into another person'. But now we were sharing a bottle of Sancerre with no obvious effect on her personality, so I asked why Stephen Ward cultivated Captain Ivanov. Was Stephen, perhaps, indulging in a little espionage?

'Oh yes. Now I think so. Stephen was a Communist sympathizer. He once told me to ask Profumo when Germany was going to get the bomb.'

'And did you?'

'Of course not.' Miss Keeler's voice was still gentle and low, and she answered with a small smile. 'Did he honestly think I'd ask a question like that?'

I believed her. An article of her faith would be to soothe and not irritate any man she was with, even if he did happen to be Secretary of State for War.

'But you did have an affair with Ivanov?'

'I didn't mean it to happen but it did. It was on the night I met Jack Profumo.' Saturday 8 July 1961 was the fatal date for the participants in this almost-forgotten drama and the place Lord

Astor's house at Cliveden, where Stephen Ward was entertaining the Russian Attaché and Miss Keeler at his cottage in the grounds. It was there that the War Minister saw Miss Keeler splashing in the pool and being deprived of the swimsuit she had left on the side by laughing companions. Not since David spotted Bathsheba in a similar situation has so much trouble been caused by an act of observed bathing.

'That night Ivanov drove us back to London and he had a bottle of vodka in the car. We got rather silly and that's when it happened. Jack Profumo rang me up soon after that. He was a bit overpowering, not really exciting. I think I saw him about four or five times. He gave me a lighter and a bottle of perfume and £25 for my mother. We never went out to a restaurant together or anything like that. Then he told me I must leave Stephen or he wouldn't see me any more and I didn't want to leave Stephen.'

Events were moving fast in the lives of the two participants in this brief and somehow meaningless affair. Mr Profumo was in some trouble with his political masters and Miss Keeler with two black men, Lucky Gordon and Johnny Edgecombe. It seems that Stephen Ward wanted a black girlfriend and with some sense of furthering this design Miss Keeler met a man called Lucky Gordon in a coffee bar near their flat. She visited Mr Gordon who, it seems, raped her and, on a subsequent occasion, beat her up. She also met Johnny Edgecombe, a man of jealous disposition, who carved up Lucky Gordon's face. 'I didn't ask him to do it,' Miss Keeler explained as I poured her another glass of Sancerre, 'it just ended up like that.

'I had bought a gun when I was living with Johnny Edgecombe in Brentford. It was a revolver with seven live shots in it. I bought it from a friend. I took it down to Wraysbury to show my mother. When I was living with Johnny I did sleep with men for money for a couple of weeks. That's something I haven't admitted. When I left him I discovered he'd taken my gun. I went back to Stephen's flat because I'd decided to pull myself together and get a job and not sleep with men for money any more. Johnny Edgecombe was very jealous; he kept ringing up. Then he came round. I was in the flat with a girlfriend and he shot at the door. Of course we'd locked it. Lucky for us one of his shots jammed the bolt and he couldn't get in. My girlfriend rang the police and they came and got him. When Johnny's trial came up I went to Spain; I really didn't want to be around for that. I was there when the rumours started about me and Jack Profumo. I bought a paper in Madrid and found that I was a famous model. I was quite excited. There weren't horrible people calling me a prostitute then.'

If the course of true love wasn't running particularly smoothly for Miss Keeler, the War Minister had troubles of his own. He had been told by the Secretary for the Cabinet that the Head of Security was worried about his remote connection with Messrs Ward and Ivanov. He had been questioned by the then Attorney-General about his friendship with Christine Keeler and acquitted of any 'impropriety'. On top of all this the Labour MP George Wigg raised the question of the rumours in the House of Commons.

'I think I was really in danger when I was in Spain. I think they'd have killed me if they'd had the chance.'

'Who'd have killed you?'

'The Labour Party. George Wigg and that lot wanted to have me killed.'

The thought of the late George Wigg, MP, stealing along the Costa Brava at the head of a posse of heavily armed Labour thugs in pursuit of the girl from Wraysbury was fascinating.

'But why would the Labour Party want to kill you?'

'They had to attack the Government. They needed to prove Jack Profumo was a spy or going around with spies, and they thought that as soon as people clapped eyes on me they'd know I wasn't a spy. So they wanted me out of the way. If I'd've died in Spain it'd've been much easier for them.'

'Did you feel at all guilty, about the disaster for Mr Profumo, for instance?'

'I am guilty. I'll tell you about my guilt. When the *Daily Express* caught up with me in Spain I was with my girlfriend Kim and they told me it didn't matter what I said because they couldn't print it. So I did tell them I'd had sex with Profumo. I had heard that he had "denied impropriety" and I couldn't believe it.'

Afterwards Mr Profumo felt obliged to make his confession also, in the House of Commons, and the British Public had one of its periodical fits of morality, a spectacle which Lord Macaulay long ago and quite correctly described as ridiculous. Stephen Ward was tried on a variety of thinnish charges, including living off immoral earnings, and driven to suicide. Lord Denning wrote a report on the matter which led to the first queues outside Her Majesty's Stationery Office and *The Times* published a thunderous leader blaming the materialism of the Conservative Government for the breakdown in public morals.

'I'd broken up with Stephen. After the shooting at the flat he began to say I was a bad girl. He had changed then and looked terrible and he seemed to be after money. But when he died I had the worst attack of asthma I'd ever had in my life. And I hated people. I went to buy a paper and heard some people say, "He's dead, the old ponce." I was so furious that I wanted to kill them. I drove my car at them, but at the last minute I hooted and they jumped out of the way.'

Lucky Gordon was also tried, and the occasion was used as an outraged moral attack on Christine Keeler. She had denied that two black men were present when Mr Gordon had beaten her up. This statement was untrue and she was subsequently tried for perjury and sentenced to a term of six months' imprisonment.

'When Lucky was let off they had to get me. I was like a wounded animal. I had to take what was coming. When I went into Holloway I was really pleased to get a bit of peace. I was psychologically exhausted. It wasn't a very pleasant place but I met a girl there who's been a good friend to me. She works for the Labour Party. It was rather like being in the Army.'

'When were you happy during all this?'

'Oh, when I first came to London. I told you. When life was all a joke. And after it was all over, in the late sixties when I was a member of the jet set. Since then I've had two husbands, a labourer and a company director – quite a contrast.'

'Whom did you love out of all these people?'

'Oh, I loved Stephen. Always. I'm a very loyal sort of person.'

'What do you do now?'

'I write. I've collected all the papers about all the cases. They're in the bank. Oh, and I do jigsaws. And crosswords.'

'Do you go out much?'

'Not really. I wouldn't like men to take me out to dinner and so on in the hope of something happening afterwards, and then for them to be disappointed.'

'What do you think of the whole business, looking back on it?'

'It probably wasn't anyone's fault. It was silly, wasn't it? Silly Profumo, silly Stephen, silly me. I don't think about it a lot.'

Coming from a lady who once removed her bathing dress and caused the eventual disintegration of a Government, I thought the verdict showed a certain degree of modesty.

Three Times Happy

EDWARD HEATH

The room was light and meticulously tidy, the ashtrays all set at exactly the same angle. The walls were bright with paintings of boats and beaches. The pile of books by the sofa was topped with Edward Heath on music, beneath it lay a life of Horowitz, a work on Stravinsky and Lord Clark on civilization. There was an LP of Rossini overtures on the record-player. Lit shelves held drinks and small busts of great composers. Outside in the London street a policeman kept guard, the last vestige of ex-Prime Ministerial power.

'I haven't kept you waiting?' Mr Heath appeared suddenly, his hair greyer than I had remembered it, his voice gravelly, wearing a blue suit and holding in a large white hand, front forwards and just below his waist in an attitude of modesty, the score of Rachmaninov's Second Piano Concerto. 'What would you like?' He was smiling broadly. 'Coffee? Cognac? Bacon and eggs?'

'Coffee would be very good.' It was past eleven o'clock and I assumed that the bit about the cognac with eggs and bacon was a joke; anyway Mr Heath seemed to be laughing. So he sat and rang for coffee, and I remembered that he had once said that *Fidelio* was really his favourite opera, although he had a surprising fondness for *Così Fan Tutte*.

'Or *Don Giovanni*, but that has flaws. No. I think *Fidelio*.' His opinion was apparently unchanged.

'Because of the music or the message of freedom and resistance to tyranny?'

'I think because of the music *and* the message.'

'And Rachmaninov?'

'Oh, I'm conducting that in Israel. A young genius is playing. They're all young geniuses now, aren't they?'

'When you stand up on the rostrum and conduct, does that give you a satisfactory feeling of power? Is it as good as being Prime Minister?'

'Well, no' – the smile was still there but seemed hurt and ironic – 'I would say, not quite as good.'

'Are you happy?'

'I've only been happy during three periods of my life: when I was at Balliol, when I was at the Foreign Office, which some people say amounts to the same thing, and when I was Prime Minister.'

'Did it come as a terrible shock to you when you lost the leadership election to Mrs Thatcher in 1975?'

'You know what Clemmie said to Churchill when he lost the 1945 election? "It's the will of God." And Winston said, "Well then God moves in a most mysterious way." Yes' – Mr Heath still looked puzzled at the result – 'it came as a terrible shock, particularly when all the predictions were OK.'

I thought of the ironies of history, among them that Mrs Thatcher, sworn enemy of the National Union of Mineworkers, owed her victory to a miners' strike which defeated the Heath Government.

'What did you do after it happened? Did you go into retreat? I mean, were you tempted to leave politics?'

'Not at all. I took a week's holiday and then I campaigned in the EEC referendum. I spoke at more than eighty meetings up and down the country in favour of Europe. Thatcher made one speech; it was all she could bring herself to do.'

'You never took a job in her Government.'

'She never offered me one. I'd made my predecessor, Alec

Douglas-Home, Foreign Secretary. Churchill asked Chamberlain to stay on in the Cabinet. I was asked if I'd like to be our Ambassador in Washington. I'd already said that I'd stay on in Parliament and look after my constituency. My interest has always been in politics. They aren't the be all and end all; if you think that you're a crashing bore. But I couldn't leave politics.'

Mr Heath, who started as Teddy and became Ted, was born in July 1916 when a German airship was dropping bombs on Ramsgate. His father, William Heath, was a carpenter and his mother an ex-lady's maid who had travelled abroad and worked in a house in Hampstead. She seems to have been a gentle, intelligent and sensitive woman who took her son to church, where he began to sing in the choir and develop his taste for music. She died, tragically, just before Edward Heath was adopted as candidate for Bexley. William Heath died recently at the age of eighty-eight. 'I was always terrified of what my father was going to say to the press.' Ted Heath speaks of him with affection. 'When they asked him what he thought of the permissive society he said he wished to God it had been invented sixty years ago!' Teddy went to Ramsgate Grammar School and failed to get a scholarship to Balliol, so his father, who had started his own building business, found the money. Once at Oxford the future Prime Minister got an organ scholarship. Roy Jenkins, Denis Healey and Woodrow Wyatt were up with him and Harold Wilson was beavering away to get his First. Mr Heath's contemporaries remember him as serious, rather fat, standing in front of the fire of the JCR – of which he had become President – reading *The Times*, holding forth about college business and seeming to be older than the rest of them. He was elected President of the Union. The first period of happiness had arrived.

'Mrs Thatcher's men are supposed to be the new, populist

Conservatives, but you were the first working-class boy to get to the top of the Party. Did you feel like an alien being?'

'Not really. Balliol helped me. It really ironed-out all class distinctions, and then so did the Army.' Mr Heath became a Lieutenant-Colonel, a highly efficient artillery officer. After the war he worked for a little-publicized period on the *Church Times* (there is an apocryphal story that he translated all the 'JCs' in an article as 'Joint Committee') and then went into merchant banking.

'Wouldn't you agree that Mrs Thatcher's political achievement has been to find the innate conservatism in the working class?'

'To find the Poujadists?' He pursed his lips. 'But her lot aren't working class, really. What've we got in the House now? PR men, men in advertising. All sorts of people got selected by local committees who'd probably never expected to get into Parliament at all. It must've come as much of a surprise to them as it did to us.' Mr Heath's smile is no longer a sudden rictus which hoists his shoulders to his ears. It's become more attractive, tolerant and ironic, as he sits like an ageing Brigadier in the corner of the mess, ruefully observing that the Regiment's gone to the dogs.

'So the most concerned Conservatives were really the upper-class Conservatives?'

'Oh, yes. You could say that. Eden never had a lot of money, Macmillan was always wealthy, Churchill made a lot of money. But their position in the world gave them a sense of responsibility. It was a question of background, you see.'

'You met Macmillan at Oxford?'

'Yes. When he came down to speak. His book *The Middle Way* had a great influence on me. You've read it, of course.' I had to admit that *The Middle Way* had never been on my reading list.

'I marvel.' Mr Heath rolled his eyes to heaven in despair at my illiteracy. 'Macmillan had seen the terrible results of unemployment in Stockton. We had nothing like that at Broadstairs. And he was an anti-Fascist. We were all ashamed of the Government's appeasement policy. Lyndsay, the Master of Balliol, came into the JCR with his gown swirling and announced that he was going to stand against Quintin Hogg, the pro-Chamberlain candidate at Oxford. So we all got together to help him, Conservatives, Labour, Liberals. It was an exciting time.'

'Couldn't you do that now? Macmillan spoke in the House of Lords about a national Government to beat unemployment.'

'It's a different sort of issue. The feelings about Munich were so intense and the problem was so simple. You either wanted to fight Fascism or appease it. You can't get that sort of unity about the cure for unemployment.'

'But is there anything that divides you from the SDP, for instance?'

'The SDP? David Owen's quite effective but what's behind him? Who else has he got? I must say he doesn't seem particularly keen on letting anyone else in his Party join in the crusade.' Another of Mr Heath's ironic smiles. 'What's the philosophic background of the SDP? Theirs is really Socialism and ours is Christian Democracy.'

'Does philosophic background matter in political parties?'

'Oh, yes. That's what divides me from the present Government. When we won on the question of student grants it wasn't the Tory Party looking after its own, as people said. It was a basic philosophic principle. The Butler Education Act had decided that tuition should be free.'

'You talk about Christian Democracy. Are you a Christian?'

'Very much so. Of course, I don't believe what we've got now is true Conservatism. It's 1860s *laissez-faire* Liberalism that never was. All that telling people to "do as I do and you'll be all right" or to get on their bikes and find a job. What's the use of telling the ex-steel workers of Consett to get on their bikes? I mean, where on earth would they go to? One of my most satisfying jobs has been on the Brandt Report. We really woke up public opinion to the condition of the Third World. Well, that's one area where market forces don't enter into it. You can't tell starving Abyssinian peasants to get on their bikes and find a job.'

'What's the answer to unemployment?'

'Better organization. This Government's quite unorganized. And of course we've got to spend money on improving our roads, public works and so on. But organization's the thing. In our time, if there was a problem in the North-East, everyone knew exactly who to go to. There are some areas where Government simply has to help. In the arts, for instance, you can't have opera without proper Government patronage. The arts have always had patrons.'

'Jobs and *Fidelio*. That's what we should expect from our politicians?'

'They could help a bit more.'

'You talked about the anti-appeasers. What do you think Churchill would have made of the present Government?'

There was a silence. Mr Heath looked round the room as though he thought that one of the handsome oil paintings of *Morning Cloud* might have been bugged by John Selwyn Gummer, the then Conservative Party Chairman. Then I almost had to lip-read to get the hushed reply, 'He'd have been appalled!'

'You do a good deal of opposing the Government. What do you think of the present Opposition?'

'A shambles! Sometimes, at important debates, there are only twelve or fourteen Labour members in the House, and Kinnock hasn't learned Wilson's trick of preventing his supporters making asses of themselves. Kinnock's an attractive customer on TV but of course he's never held any Government office so he doesn't know the weak spots. In fact they let the Government get away with murder.'

'So you have to do the opposing.'

'I point out some of their mistakes.'

'You're listened to with attention . . .'

'Oh, there's always a little group of right-wing barrackers.'

'You're shown great respect by the Labour Party now. Does that mean you're shunned by your own side?'

'Perhaps a little.' The shrug of the shoulders might have concealed a great deal of pain. 'One tries not to pay any attention to that sort of thing. And one has other interests.'

'Did you admire Harold Wilson, as a politician?'

'He was able to keep his Party together. But not to any particular purpose.'

'What about other parliamentarians? Enoch Powell?'

'Sometimes brilliant, but mostly all you hear is the buzzing of bees in Enoch's bonnet.'

'Is there any organized opposition in the Conservative Party?'

'Certainly not in the Cabinet. The opposers in the Cabinet have all been eliminated.'

'So how can it change?'

'The present policies will just wear themselves out. Changes come when people bide their time. Already there's growing criticism of the Government's simplistic attitudes. It'll happen slowly.'

'Do you think you'll ever be Prime Minister again?'

'No. Absolutely not.' I was sure he meant it. There was to be no fourth period of happiness.

'What would you like to be remembered by?'

'The Common Market, of course.'

'Hasn't that been rather a disappointment? The butter mountains and wine lakes?'

'It's only food reserves for about three days. And a German Minister I was talking to had a far more sensible attitude to our selling wine to the Russians than we have. He said it was the most terrible plonk anyway. I'm also proud of the fact that my Government produced the only plan for Ireland that was agreed to by both North and South: the Sunningdale Agreement in 1973. People forget that.'

'What would you be doing now about disarmament?'

C.P.—3

'What we must aim for is parity in weapons, not superiority. Once we get parity we can begin to agree reductions. Nixon realized that. And he was by far the most successful in dealing with the Russians; he was a right-wing President who could afford to do left-wing things.'

'And now we have a right-wing Prime Minister who only does right-wing things?'

'Of course. And Reagan's the same. Thatcher should be putting pressure on America the whole time to aim for parity. But will she?' A tired lifting of the shoulders and Mr Heath answered his own question.

When Harold Macmillan became Prime Minister it is said he celebrated with oysters and champagne at his Club with his Chief Whip, his factotum, Ted Heath. Now Figaro has taken over from the Count in promulgating the doctrines of the old-style, benevolent Conservatism in which it was considered the decent and gentlemanly thing to look after one's tenants. But the estate passed into new hands and is now run by property developers with a firm eye on the market. Mr Heath may not be the most generous of opponents; he has not been lavish in his praise of Mrs Thatcher's Government, although he has said he welcomed the Hong Kong agreement – a fact which he says did not receive sufficient attention. He has laid himself open to charges of jealousy, bitterness and sour grapes; but there can't be much joy in his political isolation and there seems no reason to doubt his sincerity.

And so he went to Jerusalem. He stood on the podium, raised his baton, and the orchestra and the young genius burst into Rachmaninov's Second; satisfying, of course, but not the same recipe for happiness as conducting the affairs of a nation.

You Know How
to Whistle, Steve?

LAUREN BACALL

'You know, Steve, you don't have to say anything. You don't have to *do* anything. You just have to whistle. You know how to whistle, don't you, Steve? Just put your lips together and blow . . .'

Movie buffs may well correct her. Miss Lauren Bacall was quoting from a long memory, looking back forty-one years to the time when she caught a box of matches from Humphrey Bogart and looked up at him through long lashes, past a sleek wave of hair. She was the new girl of the 1940s in *To Have and Have Not*, the girl as one of the boys, with a cigarette, a husky voice and a joke for every occasion, who answered to the sound of a whistle, provided the whistler was a tough guy with a heart of gold, wearing a sailor's cap and an enigmatic expression.

'I just wanted to find out if that wise-cracking, experienced girl was anything like you. Please don't answer this if you don't want to, but had you had any love affairs by the time you starred in *To Have and Have Not*?'

'*Mister* Mortimer! What a question! Of course not. I was a nice Jewish virgin. I looked at Bogart in that way because I was so scared I couldn't keep my head up properly.'

'Was he really that tough character he played?'

'Let me tell you, Mister Mortimer. Bogart was an old-fashioned man, with a great pride in his profession. He really hated Hollywood. He'd been married to three wives, but when it happened I was the first time he'd been unfaithful. You know what he was?

Emotionally fragile. He lived by the Ten Commandments and the Golden Rule. Bogey was twenty-five years older than me. Remember he was born in 1898 and fought in the Navy in the First World War. Then he went to work on Broadway. He was a Stage Manager first. Then he was in a whole lot of plays where he came through a French window with a tennis racquet. Drawing-room comedies. I think it may be a legend that he was the first actor to say, "Anyone for tennis?" '

I thought of Humphrey Bogart, born during the reign of Queen Victoria, fighting in the same war as Wilfred Owen and Siegfried Sassoon, meeting the nineteen-year-old World War II girl and being bowled over. 'He was always a perfect gentleman,' Miss Bacall was saying.

'So he wasn't really like Sam Spade and Philip Marlowe – the detectives he acted?'

'Not at all. I told you, he was a perfect gent.'

'Why do you think he's lasted so well? More than Clark Gable or Gary Cooper, he's still the hero of the young.'

'Well. He did noble things.'

What sort of noble things, I wondered, did Mr Bogart do.

'Well look. He didn't take money for his detective work. And when he found out his girlfriend was a crook, he handed her over to the police. It was the sense of honour, you see?'

I blinked, because it was not exactly Mr Bogart who had behaved so selflessly, but Philip Marlowe in *The Big Sleep* and Sam Spade in *The Maltese Falcon*. How to separate the play from the player, the eternal, deathless image from the actor who changes and grows old? Had Bogart and Bacall fallen in love with each other or the characters in her first movie? Probably quite a lot of both.

'Do you think you'd have fallen for Bogart if he'd run the local drugstore, for instance?'

Lauren Bacall, aged sixty, still thin, wearing well-pressed trousers and a sweater, still manipulating a long cigarette, still looking up with her head lowered, still speaking in the husky voice of the girl who can kid around with the chaps, said, 'No. Because then he wouldn't have been Bogart.'

'My father had left us when I was about five years old. I think he sold medical supplies. I was brought up by my mother. I owe everything to her. She was a secretary in New York, and a damned good one. My uncles were lawyers and good ones too. They were all Democrats. My Uncle Charlie told me I had to read *The New York Times* every day. I went to the movies all the time because I was besotted with Bette Davis. And to the theatre. I saw Gielgud in *Hamlet* and I was just *overcome*.

'I was a real Jewish banana. What does being Jewish mean to me? It means a sense of family, and character. And humour. Humour means everything to me. It's true that when we fell in love, I told Bogart I was a Jew and asked him if he minded. I'd met so much anti-Semitism. The other models I worked with were anti-Semitic. My first director, Howard Hawkes, was anti-Semitic. Mother and I were even turned away from a little hotel in Florida because we were Jewish – it's hard to believe that now. Actors are sort of outcasts as well. To be an actress makes you a bit of a freak. You're meant to be for amusement only. Not to have ideas of your own.'

The stage-struck Miss Bacall, having been voted the most beautiful usherette in the New York theatre, became a model and was seen by Howard Hawkes on the cover of *Harper's*. He took her to Hollywood for a screen test. 'Hawkes made me into the girl of his fantasies, a girl who'd been in his head for years. The character in *To Have or Have Not* was entirely his creation. He changed my name from Betty to Lauren, and I became his creation too. And then it all blew up in his face when I fell in love with Bogart. I tell you, Mister Mortimer, he was *not* pleased.'

'Didn't you have anything in common with that girl?'

'Humour, yes. I told you, humour means everything to me.'

53

'Did you think you'd fall in love with Bogart? Before you started making the picture, I mean.'

'Of course not. I didn't think he was my type at all. All my life I'd been in love with Leslie Howard.'

It was the middle of a hot afternoon and we sat in a dressing-room in the Theatre Royal, Brighton. As I had come in through the Stage Door, I had heard the disembodied voice of Harold Pinter directing a technical rehearsal of Tennessee Williams's *Sweet Bird of Youth*, on its way to the West End with Lauren Bacall.

She sat up very straight in front of her mirror, beside her vases of flowers, and lit another cigarette to remember the early days of a clandestine affair. There was the time when she had hidden from the violent, hard-drinking third Mrs Bogart, in a lavatory on a boat, and one of the Ten Commandments had, I suppose, gone bust. Then she had married and enjoyed eleven years of great happiness and two children before Mr Bogart's untimely death at fifty-seven. 'The good guys are the ones that get killed.' Lauren Bacall remembered the horrors of that last, long illness; the final agony of seeing her husband, the great star, being taken away by the morticians in a sack. 'And the shits live on. God doesn't manage things very cleverly.'

'Was Bogart a male chauvinist?'

'He thought women should work. But he did say his ideal was to have a very small woman he could keep in his pocket and bring out occasionally. If she talked too much he could just put her back in again.'

I heard the sound of a great future rustling, outraged feminists throwing down this interview at the notion of pocket-sized women.

'And drink . . .?'

'Bogey learned to drink in the prohibition era. That's when his friends, writers like Bob Benchley, learned to drink too. It got a bit better after we were married for a while. But he had to have cocktails, lethal Rob Roys, before dinner – one was too many and two weren't enough for him. He drank beer with dinner, and then lots of Drambuie after.' I thought of the horrors of American drinking, deprived of wine. 'Did you drink with him?' I asked.

'I taught myself to drink vodka. They don't like you not to. I mean you can't just sit there being a Judge on the sidelines. And it's kind of boring being with someone who drinks. They tend to say the same things over and over again.'

'Your second husband, the actor Jason Robards, also had a problem with drink?'

'I must like trouble, mustn't I? Of course Jason had a problem. He had to live in the shadow of Bogey. And I had had one wonderful relationship in my life already. But why *would* I do it?' Miss Bacall looked at herself in the mirror, puzzled. 'I must love trouble.'

'And love men who get into trouble?'

'I can't stand people who constantly are in control. I like people who make mistakes.'

'And Mr Sinatra?' I asked about another of Miss Bacall's more notable loves. 'Did he bring trouble too?'

'A difficult man. But full of laughter and excitement. We had a lot of good times together. He was at his peak and it's not the worst thing in the world to be sung to by Frank Sinatra. And then I said something about marriage and he wouldn't even discuss it. Frank just couldn't cope with the idea. I liked what I had of him. He was interesting.'

'Have you ever had affairs with any uninteresting men?'

'Uninteresting? One or two I guess. In desperation.' Miss Bacall laughed and then became serious. 'You know men are getting fewer and fewer, *Mister* Mortimer. There really are very few of them left.'

'In your great time in Hollywood, the war was going on. Were you conscious of that?'

'I used to work at the Stage Door Canteen in New York. It was all drama to me. Dancing with young sailors and airmen going off to fight, seeing the Lunts pour out coffee for them. But then Europe was a long way away.'

'Life in Hollywood went on regardless of the war?'

'More or less, yes.'

'After it you were quite political. You and Humphrey Bogart led a protest to Washington in the McCarthy era.'

'Oh yes. It was the drama I liked about that, the idea of a crusade. But Bogart said he'd stuck his neck out, and worked for Roosevelt, at a time when actors were just meant to be entertainers and not have political opinions. My real political friend was Adlai Stevenson. He opened corners of my brain. Because he was a loser, no one remembers the great things Adlai said. And then he died so he could never say them again . . .'

'What about America today?'

'*Mister* Mortimer. *Please*.' The Bacall eyes turned to heaven in well-dramatized despair.

'Did you know Ronald Reagan when he was an actor?'

'I remember him when he belonged to the "Democrats for Truman".'

'Wasn't he President of the Actors Union, something like that?' I asked.

'He was, and *not* a good one. He never got us a proper deal. Look at all the times they play my films and Bogey's films on television. And do we get a penny for it? Do we hell! No. Mr Reagan was not one of our brightest ideas.'

'After those first two wonderful movies with Howard Hawkes, *To Have and Have Not* and *The Big Sleep*, the parts weren't so good?'

'I was terribly miscast as a humourless English upper-class girl playing opposite Charles Boyer in *The Confidential Agent*. I had some directors like Herman Shumlin who gave me no help at all and was just a sullen, silent egoist, and Michael Curtiz, who called us all "actor bums". I was under contract to Warners, who kept sending me terrible scripts which I refused to do, so I was always on suspension. I don't think Bogart was all that keen on my working either. Recently I had a big hit in a Broadway musical, but I don't feel I've been taken seriously as an actress. Now's my big chance to shake my life up and do a big dramatic role.'

'In the Tennessee Williams play?'

'Tennessee. Ah! A sad man. A terribly shy, sad man. Not comfortable in himself. But he wrote great parts for women. People don't do that any more.'

The dresser came in with more tea and cigarettes saying, 'I shouldn't encourage your habit.' 'No you shouldn't, should you?' Miss Bacall lit up and fell silent. I asked her about her family, the two Bogart children and one Robards.

'Sam's acting now. The others are working. Steve works at NBC and Leslie, my daughter, in the Hollywood archive.'

'Do you think you'll meet some other trouble?'

'My nature is to be in trouble again. If there's a way, I'll find it.'

'Where do you live? In New York?'

'I live in the Dakota.' Miss Bacall mentioned the big ornate block of flats outside which John Lennon was murdered. 'And I have a house in Long Island. I have to work hard to pay for two homes. I have no flunkeys, no entourage. I live alone. That's difficult because you're always the extra person at any party. I've had an eventful time, but now I feel my personal life is arid, not realized. When I'm alone in the evenings I read and watch television.'

'Those old movies that don't pay any royalties?'

'Yes, those.'

'What do you think when you see that nineteen year old on the screen?

'I think she's someone else. Not me. She seems so far from the way I live.'

'You were happy then?'

'Oh yes. Hollywood was still a great place to live, full of writers

57

and all the interesting people Bogey knew. Perhaps I was too happy too young.'

'Is it hard to grow old, if you're a beautiful woman?'

'I never regarded myself as a great beauty. I was never a Garbo.'

'I don't know . . .'

'Now, *Mister* Mortimer! Please. So I didn't think about that. I must be about the only actress of my age who hasn't had a face lift.' Miss Bacall looked at herself critically in the mirror and then dunked a ginger biscuit into her tea and bit into it with determination. 'I've worked hard to earn those lines on my face. I don't want to lose them. It is tough being alone. But I build up protections. I'm quick on return lines. I always make jokes. Not that everyone always gets them.'

'What do you want to do in the future?'

'I want to do this play well. I can't think further than that.'

It was time to go. Harold Pinter came in to say goodbye and the actress facing a new shake-up in her life had to rest on the well-used couch in the old dressing-room. I tried one more question.

'What do you really hate?'

'I hate liars. And phonies. And people without humour. I can't live without humour.'

'That's more important than happiness?'

'I don't see how anyone can be happy today except a new-born baby. Once you start reading the newspapers you realize what a nightmare it all is. Though I must say life seems fairly peaceful in Brighton-by-the-sea.'

Backstage in the old Theatre Royal, where I had enjoyed many exciting and nerve-racking occasions and where there was once a bar in the wings called the Last Gulp, I left Lauren Bacall alone. On my way out of Brighton-by-the-sea, I passed the front of the theatre. The local inhabitants were queuing for tickets and on the posters I saw the face of that irresistible, vanished girl who would be there any time Steve cared to whistle.

Ever Wondered about Blood?

BILLY GRAHAM

'The Blood of Christ will cleanse your sin! There are hazards in the transfusion of human blood. It cannot be pasteurized. It may be infected with herpes! Or Aids!' A dramatic pause followed and then: 'That never happens with the blood of Christ!'

The long summer evening was dying over the Aston Villa football ground where 31,000 people, young and old, black and white – a better gate than for many a match – sat and considered, without obvious emotion, the absence of Aids from the blood of the Lord. Far away across the turf Billy Graham was a small, suntanned figure in a business suit standing under a canopy, lit by towering floodlights that gained power as the sunshine retreated. His voice boomed and charmed through a superhuman public address system, taking on a somewhat rasping tone only when he read from the slim volume of the Testament he held open.

They had slowly almost filled the huge stadium, they had joined in 'I Will Sing the Wondrous Story', they had heard Myrtle Hall from South Carolina give 'Lord Listen to Your Children Praying' and Bev Shea from Canada discharge 'It is No Secret' rather in the manner of 'Sonny Boy'. They had heard a number of evangelical jokes about the English weather. They had dropped around £15,000 into plastic buckets, causing a sound like thunder. Now they were listening to what Dr Graham had to tell them about the Aztec Indians.

'Ever wondered about blood?' he asked them. 'The life of the flesh is in the blood of atonement. When I was at school I studied Anthropology. Not Theology, as I should have done. But I learnt about the Aztec Indians. And they had a great civilization until Cortez beat them by trickery. And they practised blood sacrifice! Twenty thousand young men a year were treated like princes. Young men without blemish. And then the priest leant them back against the altar and cut out their hearts and gave their hearts to the crowd. And everyone in that great crowd tried to get a little taste of it!'

The thousands of Midland faces looked amiable and placid, quite untouched by the Aztecs' greed for a morsel of human heart. At the press table on the turf we were sucking toffees that a girl from the Billy Graham team had thoughtfully provided. I wondered, nervously, if it would ever be possible to slip away to the loo without being taken for someone who was coming forward for Christ.

It had been 'Wild West Night' at the hotel by the Great Bar exit of the M6 when I arrived. In the restaurant, reps dressed as cowboys and members of the US Cavalry were drawing on each other and firing cap pistols in a 'High Noon' contest. Waitresses in flounced skirts and chokers hobbled round with trays of shorts. Over their heads slept forty members of the Billy Graham team. They had been on the Bible trail, visited Bristol, Sunderland and Norwich, and now they had ridden into Birmingham.

In the coffee shop next morning the Rev. Gavin Reid, an English clergyman wearing a 'Mission to England' sweatshirt, instructed me gently. 'Our crowds are mainly made up from parties organized by local churches and their friends. About 880 churches in the Midlands have joined in. When the "inquirers" come forward at the end of the meeting, counsellors advise them to keep in touch with their church. Luis Palau [another preacher] gets only about a third of our numbers. I'd never have advised him to hold meetings in London. I've really given up London. The Bible Belt is in Surrey or Woking where I live, or round the provincial cities.

'Why isn't there an English Billy Graham?' I asked, and the clergyman in the sweatshirt shook his head sadly. 'I think it's a deliberate policy of the BBC religious affairs programmes,' he said. 'They don't want a "Mr Christianity".'

'I was brought up very strictly in the Presbyterian Church,' Billy Graham told me when we met. 'We weren't ever allowed to look at comic strips. My father was a small-time dairy farmer in Charlotte, North Carolina. I had to get up at three in the morning and help milk the cows. The two things I didn't want to be were a clergyman and a mortician; they seemed about the same thing to me. Then, when I was about eighteen, a travelling evangelist came to our town, the Reverend Mordecai Fowler Ham. There was a big choir and singing and he held the Bible and explained it verse by verse. He asked people to come forward and renounce their sins. I did, although I had doubts and felt no emotion. I was worried my schoolfriends would tease me about it. In fact the next day the French teacher called me "Preacher Graham".'

'But had you really committed any sins?'

'Oh, I guess I'd smoked and lied to my father. I'd never taken alcohol and I never touched a woman until I married my wife. But we're all sinners. Have been since Cain murdered Abel.'

'Did you become a preacher soon after that?'

'No, I was a Fuller Brush salesman.'

'Were you good at selling brushes?'

'Very. I won awards. Then I went to Bob Jones University and the Florida Bible Institution. I first preached to a couple of dozen cowboys. I'd prepared four forty-five-minute sermons and I was so nervous I got through them all in eight minutes flat.'

'I want to ask you about "born again" Christians.'

'That began with President Carter. He said he was born again. Then we started to get "born again" automobiles and suchlike things. The correct quotation from John is 'born from above".'

'But religion is important in American politics?'

'Statistics show that 50 per cent of Americans are in church or synagogue every Sunday.'

'Do you think that recent American Presidents are really religious?'

'I've never met one who wasn't.'

Billy Graham grinned and his smile is very appealing. He is a thin 65-year-old, his hair still fair and he has the suntan of a movie star or professional golfer. Very tall and dressed in a grey tweed jacket and flannel trousers, he sat in the offices of the Villa Park ground, flanked by silver football cups under a notice that read 'Directors' Ladies', and sipped tonic water. He moves easily and likeably down the corridors of power, flitting like some diplomatic Cardinal from Windsor to the White House and Moscow.

'Nixon?' Dr Graham began to catalogue his acquaintances. 'I've known Mr Nixon since I preached at his mother's funeral. Let me tell you something. The Soviets regarded him as our most formidable President. Gromyko said he had a great respect for Nixon. He opened dialogue with Russia and China.'

'So the heroic Watergate journalists really set back the cause of world peace?' I asked, confirming a fact I had long suspected.

'It wasn't Watergate that did for Nixon. It was the cover-up. And he had it all on tape!' The great evangelist crossed his long legs, laughed boyishly and refreshed himself with more tonic water.

'Is Nixon a broken man?'

'He certainly doesn't look like it. Nixon's lived long enough to become a revered elder statesman and he's enjoying every minute of that.'

'Republican Christian Presidents don't seem to be entirely dedicated to your rule of loving your neighbour. I mean, is there a great concern for the poor in the Reagan administration?'

'I'd rather not comment on that. I don't want to be involved in American politics in an election year.'

'But you know Reagan well?'

'Of course. I know Reagan's mother-in-law. I've known George Bush since he was a small boy. Bush's father was my golf partner. You know what I think about Ronald Reagan? He's a great TV personality and he has the marvellous gift of physical fitness. Absolutely nothing really bothers him. Whatever happens, he just smiles and waves at the press. It's a great quality, not to be bothered. Even his biggest political enemies say "You can't help liking the guy." '

'And Jesse Jackson?'

'Oh, Jesse's a good friend of mine too. He's big, you know. Over six foot five. That doesn't show on television. He's a real Muhammad Ali. Jesse modelled himself on me as a speaker. Why, he was raised only sixty miles from me in North Carolina!'

'What do you think about the Bomb?'

'What I preached in Moscow. Salt Ten is what I preached! Let's get right down to the end of the line and destroy all those terrible weapons. We have the moral ability to do so. Young people today aren't sure they'll grow up to live a normal life.'

'Do you think the English are embarrassed by religion?'

'They didn't used to be. Not in the days of John Wesley. Nowadays perhaps. You're quite ready to say you've met the King. Or a member of the royal family. You don't like to say you've met Jesus, who's the King of Kings.'

'You believe in salvation. Do you believe in Heaven as a place?'

'To me it's a place. Yes.'

'So to get there do you just have to behave well? Love your neighbour as yourself? Or must you accept Christ?'

'Both. Jesus says no man comes to the Father but by Me.' He brought the slim, limp Testament from his pocket and waved it in my direction. 'I think you know this as well as I do.'

'So it's no use being an utterly saintly Muslim or Hindu or atheist? I mean, would you let in an extremely good Hindu?'

'That's up to God. I don't know the mind of God. I'm not saying that someone in a jungle, someone who'd never heard of Christ,

couldn't get in. But if you've faced Christianity and rejected it . . .'
He was smiling at me and I was doing my best to face the prospect
of eternity far from the company of the Billy Graham team.

'How does your organization get financed?'

'There's a trust, with independent directors. No one who's a
paid employee is allowed to sit on the board.'

'Are you a paid employee?'

'Yes. I get paid $52,000 a year. If my father hadn't left me some
inheritance I couldn't do this work. I'm preaching on the Cross
tonight. My secretary has just typed me out five headings.'

'Do you get stage-fright before you preach?'

'Always. And I get more nerves than an actor because I'm dealing with eternal matters.'

'I was going with a girl when I was a young man.' Dr Graham's
deep, electronically assisted confidences boomed round the packed
stadium. 'It was puppy love but it was real to the puppy. But she
wasn't the right one for me. She wasn't right for a person coming
to Christ. So I told her one night I could never take her to buy ice-
cream with me again. Buying ice-cream was about all there was to
do in the evenings in our town. And she cried and I cried. But if
I hadn't broken that off how would I have been ready for Ruth?
God had Ruth born for me all that way away in China. She was
the daughter of a surgeon in a mission hospital. When I met Ruth
I knew she was the one. She took a little longer to realize it. Now
we have seven – no, pardon me – we have five children.'

The Birmingham crowd laughed happily at Billy Graham's
apparent forgetfulness, perhaps relieved to have finished with the
blood sacrifices of the Aztec Indians. The sky was almost dark and
a team member walked past the press table with the attendance
written large on a piece of paper. There were smiles all round at a
particularly bumper house.

Billy Graham's present visit to England was the subject of some
controversy. An article in the *Guardian* said 'Keep Billy Graham

Out'. It was replied to by the Rev. Gavin Reid in the Church of England newspaper who urged us to receive the prophet. But Dr Graham himself was unconvinced. His supporters had to visit him while he was on holiday in the south of France to persuade him to come.

Since his arrival, Billy Graham has been criticized by the Methodists, and his brand of Christianity does seem to miss out vital parts of the religious experience. There is no room for the ecstasies of the solitary mystics, the tormented sensuality of the Metaphysical Poets or the Dark Nights of Doubt.

Perhaps Dr Graham's is a religion well suited to Presidents who wave cheerfully and keep smiling at the press, even though the Garden of Eden has become an arena for germ warfare and genocide. It's a religion that clearly goes down well in our unpublicized English Bible Belt, those packed suburban churches where no one has a word of criticism for the Miracles, or the Immaculate Conception, and where the purifying blood is mercifully uninfected.

The Rope Trick

Sir ALEC GUINNESS

'I thought we might start with your schooldays. You went to Rox-borough in Eastbourne?

'Oh, start before that. Start at the Prep School where I was dumped at the age of six. They had a sort of initiation ceremony. New boys were made to drink from a loving cup, only it turned out to be a brimming po.'

'I was ill for a year after that. The school said it was because I'd eaten a bad ice-cream sundae, but I knew I hadn't. Of course I didn't like being ill for a year, but children accept things, don't they?'

Sir Alec Guinness, seventy years old and just home from filming *A Passage to India*, balding, putting on weight, smoking a good deal, was dressed in comfortable sweater, a pair of old trousers and a checked shirt. He has a face that can change like the April weather. At moments he looked like a grumpy, retired military man out for a blow on the prom, but within seconds his face becomes saintly and innocent, like Father Brown, or hooded and slightly malignant, like a particularly refined Cardinal at the time of the Inquisition. Often, and even when he spoke of the poisoned chalice which he quaffed at the age of six, his mouth turned up at the corners, his eyes glittered, his ears seemed pointed and he became a cheery lad and, once again, Mr Herbert Pocket, the pale young gentleman in *Great Expectations*. But even at his most boyish his voice was deep, perfectly modulated and precise – low cello notes which added an unexpected dignity to the horrors of the Prep School dorm.

'Do you remember your first visit to the theatre?'

'Oh yes. A lady at the hotel in Cromwell Road where I was staying took me to music hall at the Coliseum and I fell in love with Nellie Wallace. She was an extraordinary comic, in loud tweeds and boots, with a long feather in her hat. She was hideous as a parrot and every time she bent over to pick something up the orchestra blew an enormous fart.'

'Did she make you long to be an actor?'

'No. She made me want to be a clown.'

'When you were a child you lived a lot in hotels?'

'Oh, always in hotels. I made great friends with chambermaids who brought up hot water and had a lot of fun working hydraulic lifts. My mother was with me *some* of the time. At school I used to do plays in my little cardboard puppet theatre. I wrote them myself, and they were very sophisticated pieces about titled people. I made a great hit in *Macbeth* as the messenger because I took the precaution of running three times round the playground before I made my entrance so that I could deliver the news in a state of exhaustion. Of course I always wanted to be an actor, but it was quite a long time before I discovered that acting was something you got paid for.

'By the time I was fourteen I'd really severed all connections with my mother. The headmaster of Roxborough was very kind to me; he knew someone in advertising and got me a job as a copywriter at an agency in Lincoln's Inn Fields. The money put aside for my education had really run out. I got paid a pound a week, later it went up to thirty shillings, and I wrote about Rose's Lime Juice and radio valves, subjects which I knew nothing about whatever. I spent all my money going to the theatre. You could get into the gallery at the Old Vic for threepence or sixpence, and I lived on sandwiches and apples which my friends gave me at work. Then I heard about the Leverhulme Scholarship at RADA and I paid a pound to go in for it. They sent me some audition pieces. I had no idea at all how to do them.'

Whether his courage was due to starvation, or to a certainty of his destiny, or to the fact that anyone who could survive an English Prep School in the twenties had nothing left to fear, the young Alec Guinness did an extraordinarily brave thing about his RADA entry. He telephoned John Gielgud, then at the height of his fame as a romantic actor, and asked the Crown Prince of the Classical Theatre if he would teach him how to do audition pieces.

'I think John mistook me for some well-off member of the Guinness family. Anyway, he was very polite and said he was really too busy but, "Why don't you ask Martita, dear boy. She needs the money." So I telephoned Martita Hunt and I think she also thought I was a rich Guinness. She told me to come round to her chic flat in Knightsbridge.'

I remember Miss Hunt as an eccentric, elderly actress playing the Mad Woman of Chaillot. When young Guinness from the advertising agency knocked at her door and was let in by her French maid, she was an elegant woman in her thirties lying in the bath. 'She bubbled away at me,' he remembered, 'through the half-open door, and asked me to fix her a dry martini! I had absolutely no idea what a martini was but I thought it had something to do with gin. I looked at the gin bottle and thank God it was empty, so I was never put to that test. When she emerged from the bath Martita Hunt said she'd teach me for a pound an hour, so I went away and borrowed the money. You know, I don't think she taught me a sausage, but somehow she formed my taste in acting for all time. She taught me what to admire.'

'What's that?'

'Simplicity. Purity. Clarity of line.'

'Is that what John Gielgud had?'

'Vocally he had it absolutely. Sometimes the movements could get a little strange. You know, Martita was enormously kind? She used to take me to dinner at Pruniers, with wonderful white wine and so on.'

'She was rich?'

'Oh no. She borrowed the money. One day, after I'd been going to her for a while, I came in and she was talking on the telephone. She put her hand over the mouthpiece and said, "You'll find your ten pounds on the table. Take it back! You're absolutely hopeless, you'll never learn to act." '

Despite Miss Hunt's initial discouragement Sir Alec persisted and, turning up at RADA for his first great test, was told it was a good thing he hadn't come from Scotland because the Leverhulme Scholarship had been cancelled. Unable to face the laughter of his fellow copy-writers he was wandering disconsolately in the street when he happened to meet a girl he'd known on the beach at Eastbourne. She told him that the Fay Compton School was holding auditions at that very moment. He ran all the way there and breathlessly tore off the Chorus from *Henry V*, did an unlikely imitation of George Arliss as Disraeli, and Rose's Lime Juice lost a fairly unenthusiastic copy-writer for ever.

'I don't really think acting schools are a great help because you're always acting with people of your own age. When you started with the great actor-managers you may have picked up some bad habits, but I think you learnt more. Really all an actor needs is in Hamlet's advice to the players: hold the mirror up to nature, don't saw the air with your hand or tear a passion to tatters, and something I should remember "Be not too tame neither." '

John Gielgud came to see Alec Guinness's final performance at his acting school. Later, when Guinness hovered near him in a theatre, Gielgud said, quite unexpectedly, 'Where on earth have you been? I've been trying to get hold of you to play Osric in my *Hamlet* at the New.' Sir Alec was then twenty and has not stopped working since.

The early thirties were an extraordinary breeding time for

C.P.—4

actors, offering them early opportunities that seem impossible today. Gielgud had played Romeo, Hamlet and Macbeth by the time he was twenty-five and the 21-year-old Olivier had done his first Uncle Vanya at the Birmingham Rep. Shortly after Osric, a still boyish Guinness hobbled on to the stage to rehearse the Apothecary to Mr Olivier's Romeo, directed by Mr Gielgud.

'Go on. Stand on Mr Olivier's right,' the great voice sounded mellifluously from the stalls.

'He means my left, you fool,' Romeo muttered out of the corner of his mouth. Life in those halycon days was never peaceful.

'I remember John took us all out to dinner. Oh, about ten of us. And I ordered a vanilla ice, very quietly but I suppose with sloppy diction, and his voice rang out again. "There is no 'R' in vanilla ice, dear boy." He never stopped directing us, you see.'

'Whom did you admire most?'

'I liked them both in comedy. Then John had no chance to be lachrymose and Larry couldn't be heroic.'

'When you came to do your great Ealing Comedy roles, was there a comedian you modelled yourself on? Not Nellie Wallace, for instance?'

'No. Strangely enough I admired Beatrice Lillie. She was extremely sophisticated. John Gielgud used to say her comedy was putting out one finger and poking someone in the chest so that they fell over backwards and then grimacing at the audience. As a matter of fact I think that's quite a funny thing to do. I never found Chaplin particularly hilarious. For me it's always been Buster Keaton.'

'Are you an actor who needs props? I mean, there are actors who don't come alive until they've found a pair of shoes, or a moustache, a walk or an accent. And some just use themselves. Which are you?'

'It's a help to start with some sort of prop. But I don't believe that's the right way. In the Olivier–Richardson season at the New after the war, the place became a hot-bed of false noses and I think that's too easy. Don't rely on a false nose or whiskers when you're playing the Apothecary, *become* the Apothecary. When you look at the performers I most admire – Eileen Atkins, for instance – you see it's all done from inside. You have to change yourself, alter your personality to be the part. Of course, that's far more difficult and it can be dangerous. You're playing about with your individual soul.'

'Have you ever felt you were putting yourself in danger by acting?'

'Only once really. When I played Abel Drugger, the little tobacco-maker in Ben Jonson's *The Alchemist*. He's such an extra-ordinarily innocent character. I felt as though I could go on acting him all my life and never escape from him.'

At some time in the heyday of the British theatre, Alec Guinness married Merula Salaman; she was the tiger and he was the wolf in a French play in which John Gielgud acted Noah. The Guinnesses live in a house they built near Petersfield, with a paddock, daf-fodils, and a square Japanese-style pond with a fountain enclosed by a tall hedge, where he learns his lines, a task all actors find harder and harder as the years go by.

'Tell me about God.'

'When I was at school I was troubled about a lot of things. The ichneumon-fly. Things like that.'

'You mean the cruelty in nature?'

'Yes. I got up from my confirmation practically an atheist. Then, when I was playing Hamlet, a priest called at my dressing-room and told me I was crossing myself in the wrong way. He called the next week and he told me I was still doing it. Then, at the begin-ning of the war, I went to play in *Thunder Rock* in Bristol. When I got there the theatre was bombed and I was standing with my suitcase, feeling rather lost, and I asked a policeman where I could spend the night. He told me to try the house by a Roman Catholic church, and there I found the priest who'd told me I crossed myself in the wrong direction. I stayed with him for four days. He had a very good cellar. He made a pass at me, of course, but I found I could cope with that and he talked and he amused me. He started me reading things like *The Life of St Teresa*.

'Then I got to know Catholics like Arthur Waley and Edith Sitwell. Twenty-seven years ago I bicycled off to a church near here and asked to speak to the priest. I thought, if he turns out to be a sort of Begorra Irishman I'll pretend I'm lost and ask the way. But when I saw him he was a man I thought I could trust. Our whole conversion was quite casual but workmanlike. It seems to suit my temperament.'

'But what about the ichneumon-fly?'

'Oh, I came to the conclusion that the ichneumon-fly is rather small and really doesn't matter.'

'What about death?'

'I always expected to die at sixty-four. I hope to die in what they call a State of Grace. With everything in order.'

'Do you think you'll be judged?'

'Oh dear. I hope not.' He grinned and became boyish again, a pale young gentleman. 'Of course I judge myself all the time. Ours is a silly business really. Aldous Huxley said that no actor could be a good man or lead a spiritual life. Sybil Thorndike, who was a good woman if ever there was one, didn't agree with that.'

'What did she say?'

'She said it was esoteric rubbish.'

He had promised me a 'scrap lunch' but we had smoked salmon and a Fortnum & Mason's pie he had brought back from London, with Merula and Matthew, their son. Alec Guinness smoked a good deal, we drank white Rioja, and he said, 'You know, the most difficult part I ever had to play was to be an officer and a gentleman for three years in the Navy.' And then we got back to the real business of acting.

'I remember Michel Saint-Denis, the French director, doing

The Cherry Orchard and Marius Goring walked across the stage as Yepihodov, a character whose boots squeak. Saint-Denis said, 'What's the matter, Goring? Your boots aren't squeaking!' And Marius said of course they weren't, he was rehearsing in gymshoes, something like that. So Saint-Denis, who was a great actor, got up and walked across the stage and I promise you, you could hear his shoes squeak. They didn't squeak, of course, but you could hear them.

'One other thing. In *The Seagull*, directed by Komisarjevsky, I played a workman putting up the little theatre at the start of the play. Peggy Ashcroft came back from lunch during rehearsals and said she'd been arguing with Komisarjevsky about whether I pulled a rope. He said I did, but in fact there wasn't a rope. You see, I'd made him see a rope that wasn't there.'

He walked with me to my car. 'It was so quiet here,' he said, 'and now they're going to put a motorway eighty yards from our front door.' Until it comes he can stand between his hedges, by his Japanese fountain and, learning his lines painfully, think up new versions of the rope trick.

A Broad Grin and
a Second-hand Cortina

NEIL KINNOCK

Extensive redecorations and repairs were taking place round the recently elected Opposition leader's office. I was led there by Miss Patricia Hewitt, born in Canberra, late of the National Council for Civil Liberties, and narrowly defeated candidate for Leicester East. After this setback she decided that what was needed was a reorganization of the Labour Party and came to work for Neil Kinnock.

Miss Hewitt had brightish blue stockings and a welcoming smile. She took me into the Shadow Cabinet room to drink coffee and wait in a silent place that once rang with the hammer-blows of Party Splits. We gossiped a little on such subjects as the new Police Bill.

'The last time I was here,' I said, 'at the end of the Michael Foot regime, there was a pair of high-heeled shoes on the filing cabinet.'

'Well,' Miss Hewitt said firmly, 'you won't see anything like that now.'

And then we were in an outer office. Leaning against a wall was an unexpected ecclesiastical object, a board crowned with a fretted wooden Gothic arch, fitted with sliding panels in which the numbers of hymns might be slotted. Where had it come from, this gentle relic of some distant chapel in the valleys, soon, apparently, to be hung in the Labour leader's headquarters?

It was a birthday present, from Mrs Kinnock to her husband. 'We're thinking of using it as a scoreboard,' one of the ladies in the outer office said, 'to put up Neil's marks against Thatcher at Prime Minister's question time.'

'You've met her across a crowded dispatch box,' I said. 'As you're locked together in that sort of formalized duel, do you get to have a sneaking respect for Mrs Thatcher? Some sort of rapport? Does an affection spring up?'

Mr Kinnock was not smiling. His head went sideways and downwards. He had the sort of expression that might go with the words 'Nah' or 'Come orf it'. 'No sneaking respect,' he said. And his Welsh accent was less mellifluous than usual. 'She retreats into stylized arguments. She has the references of a five- or ten-year-old child. Her answers seem contrived and over-rehearsed. I don't rate her highly at all.'

I recalled Mr Tony Benn, who might be regarded as a more pugnacious politician than Mr Kinnock, speaking of Mrs Thatcher with gallantry as a woman who protected the rights of her constituency as he hoped he protected his. I thought of Michael Foot's bewilderment at a lady who had probably never read Hazlitt. Mr Kinnock's reaction was different. He had lost his boyish and attractive smile, the answer was no longer gift-wrapped in layer upon layer of packaging words. Somewhere, it seemed, was an opposition leader who might, given the opportunity, go for the jugular. He might just possibly win.

'Are there any sorts of Tories you like?'

'None I'd be prepared to go out for a pint with.' Now he was smiling again; his accent was musical and full of charm. 'I suppose the Biffen type is the most bearable. I don't have much time for brutal simplistic Tories or opportunist Social Democrats. They're not nice people to have at your place of employment. They'd be just as unpleasant if we were all working in a jam factory.'

'You've been called the first working-class Labour leader since Ramsay MacDonald.'

'I suppose I've got the right credentials. Son of a disabled miner and a district nurse. Born in a rented bed-sitting-room. Then we moved into a terraced house.'

The house was in Tredegar, near the colliery. His father suffered from dermatitis and had become a labourer. Money was not plentiful but Neil Kinnock was an only child, the pride of a devoted, highly intelligent mother who kept him always neatly dressed, and he doesn't complain of their poverty.

'The other Labour leaders, I mean, Attlee and Gaitskell, were obviously middle class,' I said, 'but Harold Wilson . . .'

'Wilson? Wasn't his father a chemist or something?' The new leader looked inquiringly at Miss Hewitt, who had stayed with us to take copious notes on House of Commons stationery.

Neil Kinnock sat in his neat grey Marks & Sparks suit and tie, manipulating a pipe with a long metal mouthpiece, no doubt designed for hygiene. Labour leaders seem to have replaced popular novelists as archetypal pipe-smokers, but with Mr Kinnock the mouthpiece never had time to get between the teeth.

'Both my parents died in 1971. Would they be surprised to find me leading the Labour Party? My mother wouldn't. She was the greatest influence on me. I think my father would've been surprised. He was a very private character. Very calm. His politics were absolutely mainstream Labour. I suppose I was the first generation in the family to make the transition . . .'

'Into the middle class?'

'Well, the transition. I thought I might be a lawyer, or a journalist, or a politician, even a priest at one time. My mother was very religious. Being a politician seemed a job like the others.'

'They didn't want you to be a miner?'

'I wanted to. Or go into the coal industry somehow. But my father and mother simply wouldn't tolerate it.'

' "The lad's never going down the pit"?'

'That's right.'

'Doesn't that strike you as odd, though? Every miner seemed to say, "My son't never going to work underground," and yet now the miners are marching and fighting and abusing each other for the right to do just that, to work in a job no one wanted their sons to do.' Neil Kinnock's leadership was beginning in a time of trouble for the Labour Party; a long, unsuccessful and occasionally violent miners' strike was being badly led by an increasingly unpopular Arthur Scargill.

'There were miners who enjoyed the craft, miners of every generation. But the strike now is primarily for jobs. They can't just shift to any old job, you know. Unemployment's up to 21 per cent in the Welsh valleys. They see the pits as their only security. I grew up in the 1950s and early sixties. It was a much better time. A more confident time. At school we all assumed we'd get a job, which seems incredible now. None of us thought for a moment that we wouldn't find jobs away from the pits.'

'Your father was a miner and now the miners' strike is losing you popularity.'

'Some popularity. The polls are only accurate to within three points.'

'And isn't Mr Scargill your first piece of really bad luck?'

'I'd say the bad luck was the closure programme. The miners can't face unemployment. They feel defenceless.'

'Oughtn't the Labour Party to come out in favour of a miners' ballot? To do you justice you've said that a ballot is necessary to make the strike "cohere". But your National Executive has backed the strike without a ballot. Doesn't that make the Labour Party look undemocratic, and isn't it making you unpopular with the middle-of-the-road, anti-Conservative voter?'

'The Labour Party can't make demands of affiliated authorities like the NUM.'

'But if Labour were in power and there were a miners' strike . . . If *you* had the power to order a ballot?'

'We wouldn't. The Government hasn't ordered a ballot. And if there were a Labour Government we should be investing in the development of the coal industry. We have an affinity to coal.

We'd deal with the problems by early retirement, a change in the financial structure, a new fuel strategy and production targets. We should see coal as a substantial fuel. Of course, in five years there may be fewer coal mines and fewer miners. But we should offer civilized and acceptable alternatives, alternatives which would gain acquiescence. Under a Labour Government the present situation in unimaginable.'

'But Mitterrand and the Socialist Government in France is facing strikes and a mass revolt by its supporters because it's had to cut down the steel industry. Is there really an answer to whole areas of industry being run down?'

'Civilized and acceptable alternatives,' figured once again in Mr Kinnock's lengthy answer. It was as if the words had become an article of faith. It is possible, I suppose, that they might offer a glimmer of hope to the abandoned areas of Wales and the North.

His wife, Glenys, whom Neil Kinnock met when he'd won a place at University College, Cardiff, is the other woman whose guidance propelled him to stardom. He studied oratory by listening to Nye Bevan, whom he never met, but his political life was governed by a friendship with Michael Foot; to him he remained, even in the darkest days of the last election, consistently and attractively loyal.

'You met him as a nearby MP. How long? Twenty-one years ago? Was it a father and son relationship?'

'I don't think so. Michael exuded kindliness and honesty. I found his views politically attractive.'

'What did he give you? A taste for Byron?'

'Not really. Out of the two of us I was the natural pedagogue. As often as not we talked about football. Did Michael lose us the last election? No, it was the internecine strife in the Labour Party which lost us the last election.

'If he'd been at the head of a united Party Michael would have been seen as an attractive and convincing leader. The splits and quarrels made him look weak. I don't think Denis Healey could have done much better. Given the chaos in the Party, electors would have denied their confidence to Denis as well. Jim Callaghan's intervention against our line on disarmament didn't help. I couldn't understand his doing that because he's such a Party man. But again, if we'd been united, we could have shrugged it off.'

'Does a Labour leader have to start out on the left and then move gradually to the right?'

'I've always stayed in the same place. I've always been on the left and I still am. But I've had the simple premise of not mistaking a personal prejudice for a mass movement. I believe our problems, underemployment and so on, require radical solutions.'

'Does Tony Benn's return as the member for Chesterfield present you with a challenge?'

'Not a challenge at all. Of course, Tony's everyone's *bête noire* . . .'

'But you find him rather charming?'

His grin was amiable but uncommitted, and as no answer came I tried another question.

'Is a Labour leader's nightmare problem to capture the moderate voters without alienating the left-wing enthusiasts?'

'I don't see it as a problem. What I see we have to do is to explain just how a Labour Government is going to benefit the nation. Voters have got to be asked to make a decision which may be against their personal interests for the sake of a just society and a welfare state.'

'But can the Labour Party *ever* be united?'

'We were in 1945 and 1964. I've been reading what Attlee said about the Party before the war. There were the same splits then, the same tendency to adopt causes to the exclusion of the general requirement. There were splits over disarmament and between those who believed in parliamentary progress and those who thought it could be done by a general strike.'

'Perhaps the war united the Labour Party,' I said, thinking that this was a somewhat desperate remedy.

'The process started before the war,' said Mr Kinnock. 'It's started again. Of course, we've got to get more people voting Labour.'

'Haven't you lost the young?'

'As a matter of fact in the last election we got a larger share of young voters.'

'And the intellectuals, now that all the angry young men have become crusty old blimps?'

'I think all the angry young men were pretty right-wing anyway. They were against everything. They had no discipline.'

'Isn't the only way you'll ever change this Government for you and the Liberals and the SDP to get together? At the moment you're all just splitting the anti-Tory vote.'

'It'll never happen. If it did we'd end up with diluted policies. We've got to convince more people that the middle parties have no centre or substance. They don't provide an opposition to Thatcherism.'

Unlike his hero Nye Bevan, whose tastes ran to champagne and farmhouses, Neil Kinnock lives simply in a house in Ealing with Glenys and the two children, and drives a second-hand Cortina which once got clamped and so made the front pages. No doubt the story did Mr Kinnock little harm. It's hard to imagine Mrs Thatcher standing helplessly by a clamped Cortina like the rest of sinful, suffering humanity. Glenys and Neil go to the theatre whenever they can, he watches rugby football and is addicted to comedians.

'Which exactly?'

'Russ Abbott. I loved Tommy Cooper.'

Was there a doubtful glance from Miss Hewitt? Is a future Prime Minister meant to admire a late, greatly loved comic whose speciality was muffing his conjuring tricks?

'And David Copperfield – the comic, not the Dickens character – and Tracy Ullman, of course. *Three of a Kind . . .*'

'Norman St John-Stevas said a good politician must always have something in his life that's more important than politics. What's more important to you?'

'The family. Always the family. Sometimes I envy people with self-contained professions, like doctors, for instance. There is a danger of obsession overtaking politicians. Politics squeezes out other interests.'

'Are you happy?'

'What do you mean exactly?'

'Did you want to be leader?'

'No rational person sets out to be leader of his Party. It's not like wanting to be an engine driver. But if the time and opportunity come, well, you have to think about it.'

'But you want to be Prime Minister?'

'Oh, yes. That's different.'

Neil Kinnock is no doubt extremely likeable. He is everyone's favourite best man: the best at organizing the guests, the maker of the funniest speech, the first to kiss the bride. But will he ever win the hand of the Great British Public? In spite of the bubbling optimism round his office, with 120 seats to gain his task seems herculean and, to many observers, impossible. 'If you lost the next election,' I asked him, 'do you think you'd still be leader of the Labour Party?'

There was a pause then, and the longest silence since we had met. He looked quite stuck for an answer and then he smiled and said, 'Do you know, honestly, that possibility hadn't occurred to me.'

Driving up Whitehall, away from the Commons, I noted the sentries wearing their scarlet and bearskins, and a black teenager in white shorts roller-skating slowly backwards through the traffic. England has changed enormously since Nye Bevan made his passionate, mocking speeches and introduced the Health Service. The extremes are still there, the Life Guards and the unemployed. But who is going to drive down the middle of the road? Much can happen in four years, the miners' strike will be forgotten, and nobody should take a bet that it just might not be Neil Kinnock with a broad grin and a second-hand Cortina.

The Flight from Suburbia

BOY GEORGE

After a lifetime acquaintance with some fairly dotty Judges, not a few lunatic lawyers, a smattering of eccentric businessmen and pop-eyed politicians, it was refreshing to take a cup of morning coffee with a chap who is articulate, reasonable and possessed of a robust common sense. The fact that the chap in question appeared to be got up as Madam Butterfly at eleven o'clock in the morning came as no particular surprise to me. After all, I have been used to carrying on conversations across crowded court rooms with elderly men in scarlet, fur-trimmed frocks and white curly wigs. As a one-time barrister I know about the irresistible attractions of dressing up.

'My mother was Irish and a Catholic. My father was a builder. I had three brothers and a sister. We were brought up with strict Christian values. Little boys should be seen and not heard. I was a very normal child. Loved Christmas, that sort of thing. But I would say that from an early age I was dedicated to being an adult.' Boy George talks very quickly and smiles a lot, as though eager to explain the jet black wig and glossy lipstick. The lower half of his body is further removed from the well-known Japanese geisha; dark blue trousers encase the solid thighs of an Irish footballer and it all ends in sandals and socks.

'I'm not decadent,' he assured me. 'I think you can make any-thing look decadent. Decadence is like Hare Krishna, an escape from reality. It all happened to me quite naturally. I went to

Eltham Green High School in South London. That's E,L,T, Haitch, A,M. Very suburban! And they were all talking about sex and cars and the TV they watched. Well, I never watched TV. I was always out of doors. I was an outsider. Not a chameleon. I did a lot of travelling. That's how you learn things.'

'You travelled?' I asked, imagining that the young George Alan O'Dowd had shipped as a cabin boy on a tanker bound for Hong Kong.

'On a Red Rover bus ticket. You remember you could do that for 50p? I went to the West End and just wandered around the clothes shops and that. I couldn't wait to get away from suburbia. My mother was very, very suburban. She couldn't tell one end of Bond Street from another.

'Well, it was the seventies. Young people all looked like surrogate editions of Marc Bolan. Platform shoes. You remember? I wanted to be different. I had fair hair then. I got the inside of a felt pen and coloured it blue. My father was mad. I think I was just trying to create drama, you know. Even at school, I was a bit of an Edith Piaf. I could start a riot in an empty house! And I do believe that, from an early age, I strove to be famous.'

We sat in the tastefully furnished basement flat of the girl who did publicity for his record company. Boy George had recently refused to contribute to the Life in the Day page of the *Sunday Times* magazine. His days, he said, were far too dull: just getting up, working hard, watching TV and going to bed early. Although he sings in a sweet Irish voice and writes reasonably good lyrics, although Culture Club's albums have sold 10 million copies worldwide and the group, who share all the profits equally, are now millionaires, his roots are not in music but in the simple, stylist world of dressing up. 'George was first noticed around the clubs,' the press girl of Virgin Records said. 'What was he doing?' I asked. 'Singing?' 'No. Just posing.'

'I was going with a girl called Tracy when I was at school,' he went on. 'She was a model for Vidal Sassoon. She chopped all my hair off, it was the days of long hair, and dyed it orange. My mother loved the fact that it was short but she couldn't stand the colour. She was very suburban.

'When I left school I was a messenger for a printing firm. I spent all my time in the West End. I was going with a girl from New Zealand then. Myra. She had a shaven head and fox furs. It was before 1976. Punk was just coming in. People were wearing plastic bin liners and toothbrushes in their ears. All that sort of thing. We turned up at the Lyceum Ballroom for the disco. I was with my friend Phillip Sallon. What he was wearing was outrageous! Black lipstick and a long velvet skirt. I tell you. Phillip made me look like a little fieldmouse. Well, they turned us out of the Lyceum, so that's why we started going to the gay clubs. We went to Madame Louise's, run by an old Jew in Poland Street. We found the gay clubs better than suburbia for two reasons. One was you could dress up how you liked. The other was they didn't thump you. In suburbia they thump you for anything. For speaking to their girlfriends, for anything like that.

'Later on I worked in a hat shop for another Jewish man in Poland Street. I was outrageous! I wore polka dot dungarees, long white gloves, a white face, hats, the lot. Well, I was always up late, sleeping in other people's flats, late for work, so I got sacked. Which is why I went to live with a man and two girls in an old dentist's surgery in Birmingham.'

'You liked Birmingham?'

'Oh, it was very chic, in the Rum Runner club there. But I missed my London friends like Phillip Sallon. So I came back and he introduced me to a boy called Peter. And he said, "In drag Peter looks just like Marilyn Monroe." Well, I said, tell me another. But it was true! So I met Marilyn. And we dressed up all the time. High heels. You know. Stilettos. Not dresses. I always wore trousers.'

'Wasn't all this dressing up very expensive?'

'Not really. We went to junk shops, Oxfam shops, found old theatrical costumiers who were selling up. We wore tricornes, bits of Victorian costumes. Bits of modern. Anything outrageous. Phillip and Marilyn and I. We went about like the three witches from *Macbeth*.'

I drank my coffee and thought of our world in which a curious sense of style and a quick ferret round an Oxfam shop can make you a millionaire. Then I opened a tentative inquiry into the love life of Boy George.

'I used to have sex with Tracy. Not with Myra. Later on, when I was really dressing up, I wasn't having sex with anyone. Having a girlfriend seemed very suburban. Everyone in suburbia had a girlfriend. And gays frightened the life out of me.

'I was living in a squat near Warren Street station with a lot of art students, dancers and milliners – you know the sort of thing. They weren't prejudiced. You know the working classes in England are the most prejudiced people in the world. We had a lot of fun in those days. We dressed up and went to all the parties, although we weren't invited. Marilyn and I used to hire a car and go to film premières. We never had tickets but they were always glad to let us in because of the photographs. Then I decided I had to do something. If you don't do something you can be a peacock but not a proud peacock.'

What Boy George did was to become a disc jockey in Phillip Sallon's club The Planets, near Piccadilly, playing everything from *The Sound of Music* and Vivaldi to punk. 'People came to see me. I wore straw hats with birds and feathers and fruit in them. I looked a real museum piece.

'Then I met a girl called Gabriella who was going with Matthew Ashman who played the guitar in Bow Wow Wow. I used to go round and see them and I'd sing, things like "The Black Hills of Dakota" and "Fools Rush In". He reckoned I had a good voice. As you know' – Boy George assumed a knowledge I didn't possess – 'the lead singer of Bow Wow Wow was Arabella. She was about thirteen and giving them a lot of trouble. So they asked me to sing with them at the Rainbow Theatre. I did sing with them for a little while, but then I said if I'm going to do this I want a group of my own. So I took an old room round the Elephant and Castle and started calling people up.'

'George works all the time,' the girl from Virgin Records told me. 'He designs all the group's costumes; he writes most of the publicity material. He oversees all the details. They're not like the old rock and roll bands. They're totally opposed to drugs. They don't go to hotels with groupies and throw pianos out of windows. None of that. George appeals to all ages. The ten year olds and the grannies all love him.

'The other day he went to a recording studio and a lot of girl Duran Duran fans started calling George a "fat poofter". And he said – I believe he'd say this – "I've got a better chance of sleeping with Simon Le Bon than any of you!" One of the girls tried to get into his car and then lay in the road and pretended he'd hit her. If you know George you know that's not the way he treats people.'

'I try to give outrageousness a good name,' Boy George said. 'Not like Frankie Goes to Hollywood who want to give it a bad name. I'd like to change people's sexual attitudes. I'd like to do something for all the little Georges out there.'

'Have you got over the period of not having love affairs?'

'Oh, yes. But people still think heteros make love and gays have sex. I want to tell them that's wrong. And it's wrong that all heterosexuals behave like *Diary of a Window Cleaner* and that men treat women like dirt, or women want men to treat them like dirt. We all feel the same and suffer the same. Bisexuals, straights and gays, Irish and Jews.'

' "If you prick us do we not bleed?" as Shakespeare said.'

'Shakespeare?' Boy George smiled out from under Madam Butterfly's falling black locks. 'I'm not deeply into him, although I am conscious of Shakespeare. Wasn't he one of our great eccentrics?'

Turning the Century

LORD SHINWELL

This month the House of Lords will give a party, for which the Queen's Gallery has been made available, to one of its most respected and popular members on the occasion of his hundredth birthday. When he was born, Gladstone was Prime Minister, Browning and Tennyson were still alive, Karl Marx had died the year before and Lenin was a schoolboy of fourteen. Queen Victoria still had seventeen glorious years to go. Hitler was unborn, Bismarck was alive and Czar Alexander III, father of the ill-fated Nicholas II, lived like a prisoner surrounded by police and in constant fear of assassination. Such was the remote period of history when Emanuel Shinwell, grandchild of a refugee from Polish oppression, was born at 17 Freeman Street, Spitalfields in London on 18 October 1884.

It is not only the age of the fêted peer that makes the party remarkable, but his political past. He was an early member of the Independent Labour Party, an associate of Keir Hardie and Maxton; he organized a seamen's strike, became known as one of the 'Wild Men of the Clyde' and went to prison for inciting workers to riot during 'Red Friday' in Glasgow in 1919. It's the English way, after a long passage of time, to take old revolutionaries to our hearts. No doubt in Good King Charles's golden days there will be a party in the Queen's Gallery at which the ancient and tottering Lord Scargill will be greeted by champagne, canapés and tumultuous applause.

But how much was the wild man of the Clyde a revolutionary at heart? To discover this I rang at the bell of a small flat in St John's Wood where the first Baron Shinwell lives by himself, cooks for himself, sits up at night eating porridge and reading Bertrand Russell, and has strong and coherent ideas on how to save the Labour Party.

'How bad were the early days in the East End?'

'Of course we were always poor. My mother got a job cooking breakfast for poor children in a charity school. I remember how hungry they were. A lot of them went barefoot. Then my father started a small business selling clothes to seamen in South Shields. He couldn't afford a ticket for my mother to join him, he only had half fare for me. So when I was eight or nine years old my mother tied a label round my neck and sent me up North. I had to change twice and almost got locked in the train at Sunderland.

'Later my father took me to Glasgow. We lived in the Gorbals. It was terrible, one lavatory to three families and no such thing as a bath. Like most of the children there, I went barefoot except at school. Drunkenness? People were floating across the streets! My father had a little clothing shop in the Roman Catholic quarter. There used to be terrible arguments between Orangemen and Irish Catholics in the shop and I was sent out to the corner for a drop of whisky. I was always on the side of the Orangemen. I was for the Union Jack and the monarchy. When the Boer War came I was ready to fight Kruger with my bare hands. I was always a patriot.'

Manny Shinwell, Baron Shinwell of Easington, Durham, sat in a red armchair between his television set and a small table for his pipe and books. He is a little shaky now but his eyes are bright as ever and when he talks about politics his voice becomes stronger and his index finger juts out as though to prod the Opposition in the chest. I asked him if his mother or his father had influenced him most.

'Neither!' He was positive. 'My father could hardly read and my mother read penny novelettes. Romantic stuff. But I used to go to the Public Library and read everything. Darwin, H. G. Wells. H. G. Wells meant a lot to me. I've got signed copies of his books over there. I didn't care much for Plato. I liked Socrates. I used to go to the Kelvin Grove art gallery and look at the dinosaurs. I was always interested in evolution. Also I loved sport. I joined a football club and by the age of sixteen they'd made me the trainer. I went to a little gym and wanted to be a professional boxer, but my father told me that getting black eyes was "undignified".'

By 1903, when the Boer War was over, Balfour was Prime Minister and the indulgent Edward VII was on the throne, Manny Shinwell was working in a clothing factory. He joined the Amalgamated Society of Clothing Operatives and married the first of his three wives, a beautiful girl in the tailoring trade, star of Glasgow pantomimes and concerts. 'If she hadn't married me,' he says, 'she might have become a star.' He also joined the Independent Labour Party. 'I never really knew who Karl Marx was,' he said. 'I didn't give a damn about Karl Marx. I was protesting about unemployment.

'I remember Bonar Law, future Prime Minister and Conservative Member of Parliament for the Gorbals, giving a speech in Glasgow, and it was all about Free Trade or something and they were applauding him! Unemployed men were applauding Bonar Law! So I shouted out, "What about the workers!" and someone put their hand on my shoulder to quieten me down. So I shouted it out again much louder and they threw me out. I got my picture in the papers. Once you've got your picture in the papers you're in politics.'

Lord Shinwell's rise in the political world came through his work with the Clydeside seamen, his organization of the dock strike of 1911, and his job as the £2-a-week Secretary of the Sailors' and Firemen's Union. Of his political associates he found Keir Hardie dictatorial, greatly admired Robert Blatchford, the early Socialist

Editor of the *Clarion*, and was a close friend of Ramsay MacDonald, a fact which made their final split – when MacDonald formed his National Government and made peace with the Conservatives – even more painful.

'Socialism's a wonderful ideal. But it's never been realized.' Lord Shinwell gave me one of his roguish smiles, an expression which can give him a remarkable resemblance to the late, greatly lamented Bud Flanagan. 'I thought Robert Blatchford should've been able to manage it, but he couldn't. I suppose in the First War we still thought it was possible. I was never a pacifist like the rest of the ILP. I was born in Britain and I've always been a patriot. All the same, I don't think Lloyd George got it right. During the war he came up to Scotland and spoke to the seamen about "building a home fit for heroes to live in". They weren't interested in heroes. They were interested in keeping their jobs when the war was over. I used to collect crowds of seamen and take them up to London by train to sail the Atlantic. They got part of their pay in advance and they were always drunk on the train. It didn't need courage to keep them in control, it needed guts. That was what I did for the Government.'

By 1919 the Glasgow workers had discovered that peace hadn't brought about a land fit for heroes. During disturbances caused by a strike called to demand a forty-hour week Manny Shinwell was arrested. 'Remember it was just two years after the Russian Revolution and the Government was scared. Someone had to get sent to prison. Willie Gallagher, the Communist, got three months. I got five and a half and I was the moderate! The porridge in prison was uneatable. I complained to the Governor, who was a hard, military man, and he said, "You've got to eat your porridge." So I said, "You can eat it as much as you like." After that they gave me bread and tea.'

By 1922 Manny Shinwell was a Member of Parliament, and sixty years ago he was made Ramsay MacDonald's Minister of Mines with £1,500 a year and no car. 'All this talk by the Government about the mines having to pay. The mines have never paid! That's why the old mine owners were delighted to get £16 million and have them nationalized! You know, when we nationalized the mines – when I was Attlee's Minister of Fuel and Power – I had no documents, no advice on how to take them over. All we had were a few pamphlets written by Arthur Greenwood. The miners' leaders came to see me and I asked them to come in to help us manage the mines, but they didn't want to – all they were interested in was a five-day week and three weeks' holiday. They didn't want to be part of the management. The Official Secrets Act stopped me telling that story for thirty years.

'Miners used to get six shillings a shift so it didn't matter much if they were working or not. Now they're members of the middle classes with cars and washing-machines and colour TVs. They can't afford to lose all that. And that's what Arthur Scargill understands. I don't think he's out to overthrow the Government. We've always had an Arthur Scargill. In my days he was called Arthur Cook. The Government ought to concentrate on manufacturing by-products of coal and providing alternative jobs. Of course they'll have to compromise in the end, but they ought to remember there was never a time when the pits paid. Railways never paid either, except for 3 per cent of the Great Western.'

'I've been thinking about the future of the Labour Party and some of us are getting out a document. Why did we lose the last election? Because of our policies on nationalization and defence! Well, take nationalization. We're committed to a mixed economy. We need a partnership in industry, more worker participation; we need a more popular alternative to outright public ownership.' Manny Shinwell's eyes were shining, his finger was wagging and he was thinking entirely about the future. 'Defence? I've always got on well with Generals since I was moved to the War Office after the fuel crisis in 1947. Montgomery in particular was very fond of me. When our Government was defeated Monty said to me, "You've got to stay on. I'll fix it with Churchill." Attlee always said to me, "The Generals trust you." Well, I've always been a patriot, an Englishman born in Freeman Street, Spitalfields.

'I believe in conventional weapons and NATO. Well, the Labour Party's committed to NATO. As for nuclear weapons, I think we can go on with research but we needn't spend any more money on them. I think we'd get people to agree with that. Am I against the Bomb? I'm not against the Bomb. I know from my reading of their literature that the Russians are half mad. Well, their books are all about assassinations and mad things like that. I think we need to be able to say, "Look here, Russians, if you're going to do something stupid, we'll do something stupid back."

'Those are the things I've been thinking about. Policies for the Labour Party that might win an election.'

'Tell me about Prime Ministers,' I asked him. 'You had a great affection and admiration for Ramsay MacDonald.'

'I proposed him as leader of the Party in 1922. I knew the man and understood him. Then he went into the National Government and split the Labour Party. I stood against him at Seaham in 1935. I fought an ex-Prime Minister and an old colleague. No one expected me to win but I got back with a 21,000 majority. I tell you, the MacDonald family always send me their good wishes. I always got on well with Malcolm MacDonald. Sheila MacDonald came up and put her arms round me at a party.'

'Did Ramsay MacDonald forgive you?'

'Well, no. He couldn't, could he?'

'What about other Prime Ministers?'

'Well, take the Conservatives. Baldwin was a benevolent man, a generous man. I tell you what, Douglas-Home was the best Foreign Secretary I've known. Alec Douglas-Home was always a perfect gentleman.'

I felt some surprise at this judgement but when I mentioned Manny Shinwell's unlikely admiration to Charles Douglas-Home, then Editor of *The Times*, he confirmed the friendship and said, 'Uncle Alec was always very fond of Tyneside revolutionaries,' as though they might have been some rare but attractive species of gamebird.

'Macmillan was the best Tory Prime Minister I knew. Easily the best. He was very astute and he understood the job.'

'Mrs Thatcher?'

'Quite capable within her own lights. Nothing like as politically understanding as Lady Tweedsmuir, and she couldn't hold a candle to Margaret Bondfield, the first woman in a Labour Cabinet, or Susan Lawrence, who could out-argue any Chancellor of the Exchequer. They were both much better women politicians.'

'What about Labour Prime Ministers?'

'Easily the best was Wilson. His good points were that he was competent, a good debater and very well informed. His drawback was his lack of a coherent direction. I tried to help him all I could.'

'Callaghan?'

'No comment.'

'Attlee is always thought to have been the most successful Labour Prime Minister.'

'Attlee was a very reticent man, but a good man to get on with. He would never have made it if he hadn't had Ernie Bevin behind him. He made a mess of India, I mean look at the state of India now! All he did was get rid of Wavell as Viceroy and appoint what's-his-name? *Battenburg*. That pleased the Royal Family. Attlee's one great achievement was in the Korean War. He managed to restrain MacArthur from attacking China. But Attlee wasn't a well man, you know. He had eczema.'

'You knew Nye Bevan well.'

'Oh, yes. We went to Barcelona together in the Civil War. I knew our side was going to lose.'

'Was Bevan a great loss to the Labour Party?'

'I don't think he'd've come to much in the long run. He was finished when he made that remark in favour of the Bomb and said he "couldn't go naked into the conference chamber". That compromised him. Of course, he didn't lead the life he should have done, neither did Gaitskell. How do you think they came to die at that early age? It's like I said to Bob Boothby, "You love love more than you love life."

'My first marriage lasted fifty years. I've had three wives and all of them died of cancer. There's no scandal about me. None whatever. I'm the one politician no one ever accused of having a love affair.'

'Do you think we're more civilized now than when you started out in politics?'

'Civilized! You know what they mean by that on the television? It's even in the *Telegraph. Art.* Art! They're always talking about art! You know what's much more important than art?'

'What?'

'Sanitation!' Lord Shinwell looked triumphant.

'You think so?'

'Of course. Clean water. The avoidance of pollution. You could end malaria and cholera in the Third World with proper sanitation. You know, Mrs Thatcher could solve all our problems if she built us new sewers. Settle the sanitation and the unemployment issues at once, of course she could. Things are better in that respect than when I was young, of course they are. But they're not good enough.

'I look after myself here.' Lord Shinwell showed me round his small domain: a bedroom, a book-lined sitting-room, bathroom and kitchen. 'I can make my breakfast and supper. I go to bed soon after it gets dark. Then I wake up a few times in the night and make porridge. It's better than I got in prison, I tell you. And I read. You can get a lot of fun out of Bertrand Russell's philosophy. And I read Winston Churchill's *Great Contemporaries* and Birkenhead's *Essays*. I'm really quite comfortable here. I've managed to save up a fair bit of money out of my books and journalism. And I'm going to leave half of it to charity and half to my family.

I tell you' – Lord Shinwell was smiling with delight as he went to a cupboard and generously uncorked a bottle of Glenfiddich – 'some of my family are going to be disappointed.' He watched as I poured whisky into a small glass, but didn't join me in a drink. 'That Glenfiddich's strong,' he said. 'You don't want too much of that. Now you go away and write a good story.'

I said I would try. It would be a story about an old Labour fighter who has become a favourite of the Lords, a Socialist who never gave a damn about Karl Marx, and the grandson of a Polish refugee named Shinewell who became as pugnaciously, impossibly and strangely English as any of his peers.

Nicking Jung

TOYAH

There was a time within living memory when a walk down the King's Road was an enjoyable experience, a remote period of girls trying to look like Julie Christie, and Italian restaurants decorated with clean, white lavatory tiles, in which film producers in gold bangles and safari suits waved and twittered harmlessly at each other.

For some years I had avoided the thoroughfare, and a return to it came as a shock, for a journey down the King's Road now seems like a trip on the ghost train in an extremely tacky and ill-kept provincial fairground. It was not only the bedraggled, whey-faced and lethargic punks, disconsolately lobbing beer cans at each other among the push-chairs on the benches in the square; it was not even the fact that the waxwork models in the windows of the clothes shops were smoking joints; what finished the King's Road for me was the Hitler T-shirt.

It was in the window of a shop presided over by a gently smiling Indian matron. She was doing a brisk trade in chains, spiked manacles, armoured garters and such-like lingerie; clothing decorated with barbed wire and the words 'No Future' were apparently doing well. But the T-shirt had a flattering portrait of the Führer on it and the words 'European Tour' with the dates 'Holland and Denmark 1939, France, 1940, England 1940 (cancelled)'.

So, after gazing in a sort of numb despair at the unacceptable end of the youth culture, I went into the office of the Music Management company next door. Among the golden discs and soft-spoken secretaries, I found Toyah Willcox, whose records turn over about a million pounds a year and whose hair has sunk from bright orange with black roots to a kind of discreet and reddish mahogany. We sat alone in the boardroom together because out in the King's Road she might expect a united onslaught by her fans.

'These shops full of manacles and Hitler T-shirts,' I asked her. 'I mean, how can you put up with the aggression of your sort of world?'

'It's all a bit of playacting really, isn't it?' Toyah said hopefully. 'I mean, I used to wear a loo chain when I was young and that didn't mean I was a toilet.

'I was born in King's Heath, Birmingham in 1958,' Toyah said. 'My father was very prosperous with three joinery businesses. He called me Toyah Pepita; I think he liked the sound of the words. I was terrible to my mother. She didn't want me to play with the kids in the street in case I got a Birmingham accent. I was quite a violent child. I used to drink a lot of sherry I nicked from the booze cabinet at home, and from the head teacher's room at school. I was almost dyslexic, but I was very bright in Maths. When I became a woman, round about the age of eleven, I studied satanism and alchemy, black magic and Jung.'

'How did you get to read Jung?'

'By shop-lifting him round bookshops. My sister was a nurse and we both had bad poltergeist experiences. She used to see apparitions of people who died of cancer, and my father in the next room saw the same apparitions. Mum didn't believe in them. Of course, she slept in a separate bedroom from my father. My sister and I both felt we were being strangled in our sleep. At the age of fourteen I offered myself to be christened.'

'What did the vicar think?'

'He thought I was an absolute nutter. But the Bishop of Canterbury confirmed me. It was quite a thing really. I knew the Devil existed and I didn't give a damn.'

Toyah left the Edgbaston C of E college with one O-level in Music. She had been hanging around with 'bikers' in Pershore since she was fourteen and in one Maths lesson the girl in front of her told her that Nick, Toyah's first boyfriend, had been killed on his motor bike.

'Nick was older than me. Nineteen. He was very brainy. He knew all about physics and he was a perfect gentleman. I was rotten to him really. He was the first person I loved who died. Now most of the friends I met biking are dead – heroin or car crashes.

'Nick and I never had sex.' Toyah seemed genuinely shocked at the idea. 'I mean, I was a virgin till I was twenty. I've only had two boyfriends since then. I'd never be unfaithful to Tom, my present boyfriend.'

'You're against love affairs?' I thought for a moment, nostalgically, of long-past dinners among the white lavatory tiles of vanished King's Road restaurants.

'I can't abide promiscuism. Searching for something you never find. Young people are all faithful now. They're very pure.'

'But how did you avoid sex among all those bikers?'

'I just frightened them off.' She smiled, a sensible, middle-class Birmingham sort of smile which I thought she might have inherited from her mother. 'I used to foretell their futures and freak them out.'

In 1975, the 'Early David Bowie Period and just before the Sex Pistols', Toyah went to act in the old Birmingham Rep. She performed in Shakespeare and Noël Coward, worked in the wardrobe, got a part in a television play and ended up in *Tales from the Vienna Woods* at the National. Lately she was acting in *Trafford Tanzi* and returning to the house where two of her band lived, to work through the night and record all day.

She finds it hard to sleep now; when faced with the fans who wait patiently outside her home, she finds it difficult to think of things to say to them. Sensible and extremely businesslike beneath the stolen thoughts of Jung, she realizes that she can't stay trapped in a glaring hair-do and must provide for her future by acting.

Meanwhile we sat in the boardroom and I asked her about the punks on the benches outside.

'They're really quite gentle. They don't want trouble. Sloane Rangers want more trouble than them.'

'Do you care about politics?'

'I believe in education, of course. Oh, and dance, and the body perfect. All homes can be linked by computer. Music can be piped in like computer games. I mean, people will be able to answer the music back, mix it like you mix tracks in a recording studio, and dance to it. All these kids out of work, they can be into the body beautiful. Anyone can do it.'

'You don't think it would be better to cure unemployment?'

'You can't do that. You can't change society. Not without a revolution and England doesn't want a revolution.'

'What about the women of Greenham Common?'

'Oh, I support them. I'm tired of the press putting them down for being lesbians. After all, the public can choose Boy George, who's quite an androgynous person, to be Number One.'

'Do you think we're all going to be blown up?'

'Oh no.' Toyah smiled, I thought for a moment, optimistically. 'Disease will get the world before then. Disease spread by all the sexuality.' She gave a brisk, Birmingham tut of disapproval. 'Mother Nature'll sort the people out! After that we'll probably need a bomb to clean up the disease.'

And then one of the soft-spoken secretaries came to usher Toyah out of the boardroom into her car. Miss Willcox was, as always, businesslike and unfailingly cheerful. I was left peering uneasily into a future where sex is a killer and the unemployed dance incessantly to the computerized music piped into their homes, and the massacres in Beirut are no more than a sick joke on a King's Road T-shirt. Of course, by then Toyah Willcox will have left the scene and be back acting in the National Theatre.

The Luck of the Grosvenors

THE DUKE OF WESTMINSTER

It was 10.45 in the morning as I drove through Mayfair. Well-heeled Arabs were padding in and out of Claridge's. The tarts had not yet come to work. The gambling clubs were being swept out, queues for visas had formed outside the American Embassy, women in fur coats were exercising their poodles in Albemarle Street. Out in the wastelands of Belgravia and Eaton Square various aristocratic tenants were snorting over the *Daily Telegraph* and grumbling at a steep rise in their rents. I parked in Davies Street and looked with a new eye on London's lushest pastures. I was in the middle of the 'home park', I realized, the 200-acre private domain of the young lord of the manor upon whom I was about to call.

'I look about a lot when I'm walking through it,' said the Duke. 'I notice things that need painting. And shop signs – we're very particular about shop signs. Of course, it's brick and not grass but there's still the pride in ownership. I want my patch to look good.'

I had entered the discreet door of the Grosvenor Estate Office, the place where the feudal system meets the world of property development in the nicest possible way. I waited in a panelled room; the second Duke of Westminster, portrayed in hunting pink, looked down at me from over the fireplace. He was the legendary 'Bendor' who had four wives and was the lover of Coco Chanel. It was his yacht, glittering nightly in the harbour at

Deauville, that was remarked upon by Amanda and Elyot in Noël Coward's *Private Lives*.

I had time to peer at the portraits of Hugh Lupus, the first Duke, also in hunting costume, a man with sad eyes who had been Master of the Horse in Gladstone's time and had retired over the Irish question, and of Mary Davies, who had married into the Grosvenor family in 1678 and brought, by way of a dowry, a sizeable cabbage patch that is now Mayfair.

And then it was eleven o'clock and I was led, past more family portraits, to what might have been the estate office in a country house, with ledgers and leather-bound books of records, another portrait of Mary Davies, and a young man of thirty-one chained to his desk like any other eager young company executive in shirt sleeves and a tie. Gerald Cavendish Grosvenor, the sixth Duke of Westminster, Marquess of Westminster, Earl Grosvenor, Viscount Belgrave, Baron Grosvenor and fifteenth Baronet of Eaton, not only owns a sizeable chunk of London (it includes Claridge's Hotel and the freehold site of the American Embassy) and large slices of Cheshire, North Wales, the Scottish Highlands, Vancouver, Hawaii and Wagga Wagga – he has an income reported to be around £10,800 an hour.

'Do you feel guilty? I mean about having so much money?' I asked.

'Not for a moment.'

'In a time when there are over three million unemployed and thousands of families living below the poverty line . . .'

'Unemployment,' said the young Duke, 'distresses me tremendously.' He is tall and thin, rather pale with dark hair which flops across his forehead and large, dark, melting eyes filled with the sort of yearning of that undergraduate Duke who died for love of Zuleika Dobson. 'Unemployment's much more obvious in the North and I know the Government's distressed about it too. I know an MP in government near Chester and I know how distressed *he* is. No, I'm constantly working on developments which are going to provide jobs in the construction industry so I can't feel guilty.'

'Aren't you providing housing for the rich, and even they're complaining?' (Recently some discontented members of the tenantry, including Lord Thorneycroft, had signed a letter protesting at the 'arrogance of the Grosvenor Estate'.)

'We've got a lot of low-rental property in Chester. In Pimlico we've got low-rental flats, and we're developing more.'

'When you were a child did your father walk you down Park Lane and say, "One day, my boy, all this will be yours"?'

'It's a nice picture, isn't it?'

The Duke laughed, a long laugh which is boyish and attractive and, given his earning capacity, undoubtedly well paid. 'No, it didn't happen like that. To begin with it didn't seem at all likely that I should succeed to the title.'

It is true that his family history is marked by luck. The first recorded Hugh Lupus had the good fortune to be William the Conqueror's huntsman and, thanks to a creditable performance at the Battle of Hastings, was rewarded by the gift of Chester. Luck visited the family again in the shape of the Mayfair cabbage patch and, when the Court moved from St James's to Buckingham Palace, Belgravia suddenly became a highly profitable area. The present Duke's fortune came to him by a series of accidents. The great second Duke 'Bendor' never produced an heir in spite of his four marriages, and it was a cousin who never married and an uncle who died childless who brought the title unexpectedly to Gerald Grosvenor's father.

'By the time I was fifteen it did seem likely that I would succeed, but my father was careful not to tell me about the money involved. He had a great influence on me. It was stronger because he never gave me any direct advice. We lived on the estate in Ireland and my father worked hard at his silversmith's business.

'He must have suggested things to me very subtly, so that I

thought it was my own idea that I should leave school and go and work on a ranch in British Columbia.'

Departing from Harrow with a couple of O-levels, the young heir went to work as a cowboy for 'Chunky Woodyard', a chain-store owner who had business connections with the Westminster family.

'Did you get any sort of privileged treatment?'

'If I did I'd hate to think how the others were treated. It was about 50 degrees below zero. I have fond memories of sleeping in a bunkhouse with eight other cowboys, and fond memories of sleeping in four sets of clothes trying to keep warm. After that I went to do the same sort of job as a wackeroo in New Zealand.'

'And then . . .?'

'I came back to England and worked for John D. Wood, the estate agent. My father told me to do what I wanted to do. And then I worked with the Conservancy Council in Fordingbridge. I really loved that. It had to do with the country life in England; that's what I enjoy most. We never take our holidays abroad.

'Then when I was twenty-one my father started to get ill. I was called to the colours.'

'You mean you started to take over the business?'

'Of course. It meant years of research into the history and structure of the estate. My father's time had been spent in long legal battles over estate duties. He'd had an endless case about whether or not the fourth Duke had died of war wounds, which made a tremendous difference to the duty payable. All that was coming to an end so we could go into new developments.'

'Didn't the older estate managers find it difficult to accept you, the young Crown Prince?'

'I had immense difficulties. And I felt insecure. I was trying to make decisions without detailed knowledge. But they did accept me in the end. I think I grew up a lot during that time.'

'What made you grow up?'

'I watched my father die. I was with him in his room for two days. He was a very gentle man really; he'd lose his temper about once a year. It was an extraordinary experience to see someone you knew so well in a state of transition. He was probably spiritually dead when I was watching him.'

'Did he turn to God?'

'No. He wasn't a very religious man. My mother and my sisters and I took turns to be with him. He didn't fight. He used to talk to a particular corner of the ceiling as though it were my Uncle Gerald. Then just at the end he became quite lucid. He gave me a message and it was perfectly clear.'

'What was it?'

'It was private really. Well, basically it was "Look after the girls".'

'When you inherited whatever it was – something between £500 and £1,000 million – didn't you feel tempted to go off and live in the sun and enjoy yourself and forget all about property development?'

'It didn't occur to me for a moment. My father had made me understand that I was a caretaker for future generations.'

'Future generations of your family?'

'Yes. I had the responsibility for the family to continue. However subtly he'd done it, my father had hammered that in.'

The Duke is married to a girl said by the papers at the time to have been a secretary on *Vogue*. She was also Natalie Phillips, whose grandmother was a daughter of the Grand Duke Michael of Russia. I asked him if he wanted a son to succeed him.

'I really hope so. At the moment we have two daughters who are my delight. But we hope to have lots more children.'

'And you hope the dynasty will continue?'

'I hope so.' He looked sadly out of the window. 'I can't say I'm sure of it.'

'And you enjoy the work?'

'I wouldn't be sitting behind this desk if I didn't. It's so varied. We've got minerals, garden centres, land, apart from the towns.

We're building shopping centres in Cambridge now, and Gillingham and Luton. Variety's the spice of life.'

'You've complained a lot about the amount of time you have to spend on tax planning.'

'Yes.' In fact the Westminsters have shown themselves very deft when it comes to death duties.

'Don't you think tax is a legitimate way to even out social inequality?'

'I don't mind contributing by paying my personal tax. If I minded that I wouldn't stay in England. It's the tax that tries to prevent business development I hate. I call it the "envy tax".'

'Don't you fear the return of a Labour Government?'

'We survived it before. In fact a lot of property developers did better under Labour because of the public spending involved. I don't know about the New Left. That may be a different sort of animal coming; more frightening.'

The ex-game-conservancy expert looked extremely suspicious, as if some marauder might be threatening the pheasants' eggs.

The luck of the family had just (in early 1983) rung up another jackpot. An ancestor sold the St George's Hospital site in London to the Government on condition that, if it were no longer used for a hospital, it should be sold back to the estate for £23,700. So, despite the protests of the hospital workers' unions, Gerald Grosvenor received, into his private company, a large piece of Hyde Park Corner at about a quarter the price of a Maida Vale maisonette.

'We aim to restore Wilkins's original façade,' he said with pleasure, 'and then develop it into offices. We'll spend about £20 million.'

'No problem in finding the money?'

'Not really. There's still a surprising lot about.'

The weekend was approaching and the Duke would be off to Battersea heliport where his pilot, Ken Davis, would fly him home to the big glass and concrete, modern stately home his father built on the Chester estate. He'd go fishing, or out on manoeuvres with the yeomanry, or make speeches at 'do's', or work for the NSPCC or the Salvation Army, or buy Victorian pictures.

'What's the best picture you've got at home?'

'I suppose the Velasquez is the most famous, but I can't get worked up about the Rubens or the Rembrandts.'

Before he took to helicopters (bought second-hand), the young Duke flew in a second-hand Piper Apache. He was with his mother flying through a snowstorm when the engines failed at 1,000 feet and they crash-landed in a somewhat muddy field.

'If you're going to make a habit of doing this,' the 61-year-old Dowager Duchess said on that occasion, 'I must remember to bring my wellingtons.'

No doubt it was a tremendously English remark, and no doubt the quiet workings of Grosvenor Estate demonstrate a profoundly English institution, something to do with the amazing adaptability of the aristocracy or the astute choice of William the Conqueror having its effects on a shopping centre in Luton; or perhaps just, in the Great Bingo Game of Life, the inordinate luck of the Grosvenors.

The Medium is the Message

DORIS STOKES

Those anxious to communicate with the dead are advised to cross the River Styx at Lambeth Bridge, take a long drive down the Old Kent Road, past the Thomas à Becket pub, where the boxers train, and on into the surroundings of Lewisham. Down a quiet, suburban road is a freshly painted house with a garden and a patio. It's called Ramonov after the Tibetan monk who acts as the spirit guide to its owner, Mrs Doris Stokes. The tribute is deserved because, as she says, 'Without Ramonov we should never have been able to afford this house.'

When I rattled the gleaming brass knocker the door was opened by Mr Stokes, now elderly but once a sergeant in the paratroops whose own spirit guide, an Indian named Red Dawn, killed at Blackwater Creek in 1876, arrived unannounced in the matrimonial bedroom many years ago with a bare chest and wearing a white feather.

'I've never actually seen Ramonov,' Mrs Stokes told me. 'He talks in very beautiful English. When I hear my voice on the radio and I'm pronouncing all my H's, I say to myself, 'That's Ramonov talking!' I didn't know where he came from for a long time, and then I was watching a travel film on BBC television and it was all about the Table people. Ramonov said, 'That's where I come from. Tibet.' I know he must be a monk because when I'm advising young people about drink or drugs I sit with my hands up my sleeves and that must be how Ramonov sits. He's very good with drunks, he tells them that their next drink's going to taste of paraffin.

'You like this room, do you? Boots, be quiet!' I was sitting on a sofa beneath a crayon drawing of the Queen Mother when a small mongrel, twice abandoned and now rescued by the Stokes family, bounded noisily on to my lap. 'The whole house was done up by *Woman's Own*. That's why we've got the swagged green curtains. Left to me we'd've had nothing but net all the way down. They put floor-to-ceiling mirrors up in the bedroom; well, I might have wanted to see myself with nothing on when I was twenty-five but now I'm sixty-six and thirteen and a half stone and full of indigestion tablets . . .!'

'Do the spirits always behave well when they talk to you? I mean, do they ever say anything malicious?'

'Let me tell you. I was at a service at the Spiritualist Church and there was a woman sitting there weeping and saying, "My poor Jim. He's only just passed over." And then Jim came through to me. "The woman's a bloody hypocrite," Jim's saying in my ear, "she's been living for years with this other bugger." Well, my first duty is always to the spirits and to pass on their messages but I didn't want to tell the woman what her Jim had said *exactly*! So I put it more politely. I said, "Your husband knows just what's been going on."'

Doris Stokes was born in Grantham, round the corner from the famous shop where Hilda Margaret Roberts spent her childhood. Her psychic experiences began when she met her first medium at the age of thirteen and her dead father announced his presence. Her reputation grew steadily until she was so well known locally that the police sent for her to quell a poltergeist who was throwing the furniture about in an upstairs room and terrorizing a young woman. Mrs Stokes, even then I imagine, a person of some substance, stood with her hands on her hips and, when a flung book hit her in the mouth, said, 'Bloody hell. Pack it in!'

'It was a grandmother in the spirit world. She was angry because her granddaughter had got married without telling her husband that she'd once had an illegitimate child. I told the girl to admit in her heart that she'd had the baby and then the grandmother would shut up. They never had any trouble after that.'

'Tell me about the spirits. Where do they live exactly?'

'I've seen where they live. I was led there. I've seen the Halls of Learning and the Halls of Music and the hospitals where you go when you pass over.'

'Do the spirits grow older?'

'Only very, very slowly.'

'Do they wear clothes?'

'They wear exactly what they like.'

'Eat, drink, make love? All that sort of thing?'

'I don't *think* they make love. No, not that.'

'So many people have died. I mean, where is there room to put them all?'

'There have to be some mysteries we can't ever understand.'

'What about Hell? They can't all be nice people.'

'There are no flames. Only desolate places. That's where people like Hitler go. But they always have a spirit with them in case they want to repent.'

'But aren't you in some danger' – life on the other side was beginning to sound less and less inviting – 'of meeting a lot of people you hoped you'd never see again?'

The 'Spiritualist Medium', a large, grey-haired woman with the confident air of an extremely cheerful hospital matron, spoke from the depths of her clinical experience. 'Women ask me what happens if they've married again and meet their first husbands. "Well," I tell them, "you loved both men and when one died you married for the second time. I'm sure you'll all three get on very well together." '

'But suppose there's been a terrible divorce and they all hated each other?'

'Then, of course, they'll never meet.' I should have known it. Things are arranged very nicely on the other side.

'Do you get to talk to really famous people. Perhaps Shakespeare, or Mozart . . .?'

'I don't think I'd be quite up to Shakespeare. But George Orwell came through to me once. He talked in this plummy voice about Wigan and the wound in his throat and he called me "woman". I said, "My name's Doris Stokes and don't you ever call me 'woman' again!"'

'You do private sittings for people . . .?'

'Oh yes. I went to Broadmoor once because Ronnie Kray wanted to speak to his mother at Christmas. I must say he was a perfect gentleman, he wore a silk shirt and a gold watch and a business suit. His mother came through and he cried. She said something about how his father had left his money. Later Ronnie told me he'd never knocked over old ladies or children. It was all villain against villain, you see. Now he meditates and thinks about God.'

Doris Stokes has sold a million copies of her books, she appears on television ('Ramonov tells me to forget the camera and just concentrate on my job') and her Sunday night show at the Palladium is a sell-out. 'I see a light settle on someone in the audience. Then I get messages about them. At first it's just an address or a telephone number. Then I get the name of a dear one who's passed over.' She looked at me sympathetically. 'Has someone connected with you passed over from a brain haemorrhage?'

'I'm afraid not.' I felt sorry to disappoint anyone so obviously well meaning.

'Well, anyway. I put them in touch with the spirit world. Before I go on I sit in a hot bath and say my little prayer. Water always seems to put me in the right mood.'

Before I left, Mrs Stokes took me on a tour of the house. In the bedroom I saw the long mirrors and many photographs, all apparently of dead people. 'That's Jimi Hendrix,' she said. 'He's been back.'

We can't know what happens beyond the grave, although as Graham Greene said we shan't have to wait long to find out. As I left Doris Stokes's house I wondered if I should ever be escorted back there by a Tibetan monk called Ramonov to be offered coffee and digestive biscuits, perhaps, and be barked at by Boots.

The Boy in the Long Gallery

LORD DAVID CECIL

'The great homes of the past were built by fierce and unscrupulous men. There are still those sort of people about, but they don't build beautiful homes.'

'Why's that?'

'I think for all the permissiveness about, this is a puritan age. You get beauty created by those who believe in the soul and the body. Nowadays I think people believe in the body, but they don't delight in it. And they're not sure if they believe in the soul at all.'

'You grew up in a beautiful house?'

'Hatfield, yes. I think the Cecils who built it were pretty unscrupulous. But I grew up among beautiful things.'

'What did you like best?'

'Oh, all the pictures of Queen Elizabeth. And we had her stockings there in a glass case. I thought Queen Elizabeth was absolutely terrific. I was the youngest of the family by seven years, so I had a lot of time alone.'

'And you were happy?'

'Oh, very happy. My family never believed that children should be seen and not heard. My grandfather, Lord Salisbury, the old Prime Minister, always said he treated his children like Ambassadors, but one of my uncles told me he could be quite rude to his Ambassadors. My mother was very kind, very interested in good works. She read a lot to me. She read "The Lady of Shalott"; I loved that story. She read Keats; I loved the sound of the words.

I didn't realize it was about death and all that. And she read E. Nesbit aloud to me.'

'And your father?'

'He was very religious and Conservative. The whole family was very political. My father became Lord Privy Council, Lord Privy Seal I think.' At the thought of politics, Lord David looked vague and slightly perturbed. 'I can't exactly remember.'

'You're not at all political?'

'Oh, no. Rightly or wrongly, I've never found it at all hard to resist the temptation to be progressive. And what did Dr Johnson say? He said some good things.' Lord David remembered the quotation:

> 'How small of all that human hearts endure,
> That part which laws or Kings can cause or cure.'

'Your parents sound very enlightened.' I decided, to the relief of both of us, to leave the political scene.

'Oh yes. They didn't believe in sending me away to school when I was young. My grandfather had such a bad time at school. It was the age of the child you see, the time that Barrie wrote *Peter Pan*. Children suddenly became rather a cult.'

David Cecil is long-faced, intelligent, amused, with the dreamy eyes of a Victorian schoolboy reading poetry in the long grass beside the playing fields of Eton. At eighty-one he is still invincibly boyish, chattering very quickly, as though he had been left alone all day in the galleries at Hatfield and couldn't wait to tell the grown-ups all about it.

'And then I was ill between the age of nine and twelve. I spent a lot of time in bed. That was a great help to me.'

'The same thing happened to a quite different sort of writer, John Osborne. It seemed to help him also. What did you read all that time?'

'I read *Pride and Prejudice*.'

'And enjoyed it?'

'Oh yes. I just found it tremendously funny. Now Jane Austen is my perfect companion. She has good sense, good manners, good humour and, last but not least for me, she's a good Christian. Oh, and I read *Vanity Fair* then. That was a great turning-point. I was terrifically pro-Becky.'

'What about Thackeray on snobbery?'

'I was nine then. I don't think I got all the implications.'

'Were your parents snobs, would you say?'

'Not in the least.' But then Lord David gave me one of his more boyish smiles. 'They hardly needed to be, did they?'

'You grew up in those beautiful houses, among pictures and poetry. So you came to love art . . .'

'The only thing that mattered to me really.'

'Would it have been the same if you'd been brought up with no books on a council estate in Luton?'

There was a silence while Lord David Cecil considered a strange possibility. The sun flooded into the big living-room of what was once the Doctor's house in Cranborne, where he now lives alone with a housekeeper after fifty years of what was clearly an ideally happy marriage. Just up the road is the manor where Robert Cecil entertained James I and where the family still live when they're not at Hatfield. It seemed far from Luton, but the answer came at last.

'I'm sure I'd have loved art just as much, yes. But perhaps in a different sort of way.'

'You finally did get sent to Eton. Did you mind it?'

'No, I was perfectly happy. I was a little aesthete. Not an exotic aesthete like Harold Acton became, but an aesthete all the same. And I enjoyed cricket, but I was no good. I enjoyed watching it, which the other aesthetes thought was letting the side down rather. People at Eton seemed so struck with the comedy of life and I enjoyed that.

'I wrote poems rather like James Elroy Flecker, and when I was sixteen I read Lytton Strachey. He was my great revelation, an absolute turning-point. Then I realized that a biography could be as alive and funny as a novel. I wrote a review of *Eminent Victorians* in the Eton magazine, and you know Lytton Strachey actually asked me to lunch. It was rather a failure really. I expect I talked too much. I usually do.

'Now I don't think *Eminent Victorians* is quite as good as I thought it was then, but I couldn't say so. His writing meant so much to me, it would be like parricide to criticize it now.'

'What do you think Lytton Strachey's prose taught you?'

'Never to write a sentence that has to be read twice before it can be understood.'

'You got to know the whole Bloomsbury set?'

'Later. Much later, when Lady Ottoline Morrell invited me to Garsington. I was never really one of them. To begin with I was a Christian, which was something Lytton Strachey could never understand, although, of course, he was perfectly tolerant and polite about it.'

'Were they alarming, the Bloomsbury lot? Virginia Woolf always sounds pretty daunting.'

'She was no disappointment. Of course she was a tease. She used to ask questions designed to embarrass you. But they were all rather shy and gauche, except with each other. And they all thought that their attitudes were the only attitudes. As a matter of fact, Arnold Bennett was a better novelist than any of them, but they couldn't bear the thought of Arnold Bennett.'

'They were unpolitical too?'

'I never heard them talk about politics.'

'Who was the best talker you ever heard?'

'As a matter of fact, my Uncle Hugh could be very funny in a quiet way. He said of Neville Chamberlain, "He sets himself up as having common sense by being commonplace." Max Beerbohm could have wonderful timing. He asked someone how Lady

Cunard was, and got the answer, "She's hardly changed at all." Then Max left a perfect pause and said, "I'm sorry to hear that."

'I admire Yeats enormously, but he was a very enigmatic talker. He once said to my father-in-law, Desmond MacCarthy, "The music of Heaven is full of clattering swords," and Desmond really couldn't think of an adequate reply. My wife and I once had dinner with Yeats and Lady Dorothy Wellesley, and they talked all the time and never listened to each other at all. Lady Dorothy Wellesley admired Yeats, but she couldn't listen to him. Yeats was a great poet and he jolly well knew it.

'I once asked Max Beerbohm what Oscar Wilde's voice was like. I wanted to know if it was very gentle and Irish, and he said, "No, it was like a flower unfolding."

'Thomas Hardy lived near here, but I never met him. He once said that if he'd known they'd make such a fuss about *Tess of the D'Urbervilles*, he'd have tried to make it a much better book. I know that I would have liked him very much.

'When I told my father I wanted to be a writer, he said I'd better think of something else to do as well; the Foreign Office or the bar, something like that. And then I told him I wanted to be a Don and he was tremendously pleased. He had a great respect for universities.'

In fact David Cecil read History at Oxford, but when an English Don was needed he was admirably suited to fill the post, perhaps more suited because he had taken no exams in the subject. So he has spent a lifetime writing on the people he has found most sympathetic, the eighteenth-century poet Cowper, Jane Austen, Lord Melbourne, and, most recently, Charles Lamb, as well as teaching generations of undergraduates to enjoy literature. He believes, contrary to the view of the dry and puritanical academics, that the search for art begins with pleasure.

'You can't always ask what good literature is going to do them, those poor young people. That's bunkum! The Arts must teach people to enjoy; it's no good reading "Lycidas" as a sort of academic exercise. It's got to give you pleasure. It's no good trying to pretend that English is a kind of quasi-scientific subject. You can't prove mathematically that Ian Fleming isn't the greatest writer in the world, although I rather suspect that he is not. You've got to respond intensely to literature. I think that's more important than judging it. Unless you teach students to enjoy, you might as well be lecturing a collection of little Dons.'

'But is English really an academic subject? Isn't it what people should be reading anyway; I mean, what can you teach?'

'You can give students a more intelligent pleasure. Books aren't written in a vacuum, and you have to learn about a work's period like a foreign country. Words like "Love" and "Marriage" meant quite different things at different times. But if you can see the world one day through the eyes of Jane Austen and the next through the eyes of Emily Brontë, well, that's not a bad way of living.

'Dr Johnson said that the purpose of reading was to better and enjoy life, or endure it. Even tragedy can teach you to enjoy life more, learning about the serenity King Lear found at the end. I mean Lear had an awful time but it did him good, you know.'

After lunch, Lord David put on a small, beige peaked cap which gave him, more than ever, the jaunty appearance of a Victorian schoolboy, and we went up the street to see Cranborne Manor. James I, who had used the house for hunting on Cranborne Chase, sold it to Robert Cecil, whose quiet diplomacy had helped the Scottish King to the throne. The sun shone on the grey Jacobean arches and tall chimneys, on the white flowers and the Knot garden. Around the house was a great silence in to which Lord David still talked eagerly about the Cromwellian wing, about the Cecils who managed to change sides at precisely the right moment in the Civil War, about Wordsworth and his belief in immortality, about his mother, who, if alive today, would no doubt have been a social worker, about his long and wonderfully happy marriage, and about his comic inability, after so many years, to get his own breakfast.

> 'Some violent bitter man, some powerful man
> Called architect and artist in, that they,
> Bitter and violent men, might rear in stone
> The sweetness that all longed for night and day . . .'

David Cecil remembered the poem Yeats wrote about a vanished world, where the rulers had the souls of artists, and their gentler children could be left alone for long afternoons to look at the pictures in the long gallery and read poetry.

A Good Egg

RAQUEL WELCH

Raquel Welch has written a book. It is of the sort – together with descriptions of the exercise routines of other great stars, and such works as 'sane eating for grandmothers' and 'the world encyclopaedia of talking dogs' – that is likely to go straight to the head of every best-seller list. It consists of many photographs of Miss Welch in various yoga positions, and much cheerful advice on how to achieve physical perfection and enjoy life.

It will no doubt be read by countless Americans as they munch through their generous helpings of ground beef on a bun and apple pie, as they absorb their French fries and Pepsi-Colas, and wonder why it is that they don't look like Miss Welch.

The book was a two-year task for the author. 'Writing,' she says, 'is not a very healthy profession.' And she discovered it was inclined to drive her to despair and chocolate-chip cookies. Knowing something of what she means, I turned up for dinner at the Savoy Grill with Raquel Welch and her present French husband, producer and photographer André Weinfeld, described by her as a true Renaissance man. I found her to be quite small, extraordinarily pretty, and wearing a black dress that seemed to have been clawed in the front by some giant cat so that more of the undoubted perfection of Raquel Welch might meet the eye.

'Who you are,' she writes in her book, 'can be a tricky question.' It is tricky also for the ageing male interviewer to imagine life as the object of a worldwide distribution of masculine fantasies.

'Do you think men act aggressively towards beautiful women? Do you feel they resent you?'

'Timid or aggressive. But I don't consider I'm beautiful. I have a very good figure and, because I studied dancing, I could always walk well in high-heeled shoes and I have magnificent choppers.' Miss Welch displayed some glittering teeth before they dipped delicately towards the asparagus.

'But I've always been petite, not big and overpowering, so I don't frighten men so much. But I'm hidden dynamite. The camera can find all sorts of things in me. But I don't look too good if I'm in a lousy mood or concentrating on something academic. So I'm not really a *bona fide* beauty. I can change. In the morning I wake up and say to myself, "Is she going to look beautiful or not today?" '

'Is this a good day?'

'Today I think I look quite pretty.'

Ever since she dressed in skins and an attractive snarl in *One Million Years BC*, Miss Welch has been what is curiously known as a sex symbol. Didn't she, I wonder, find that an alarming role?

'You can feel real terror. Like it's a joke they're playing on you. And you can't live up to it. But what I objected to when they decided to make me a sex symbol was that they never gave me anything sexy to do. It was sort of all foreplay and no orgasm. And there was no feeling of real fantasy. It was in 1967. The time of *cinema verité*. With the old movie stars they gave them a feeling of mystery, and I think it was much sexier.'

'Could you get outside yourself, I mean look at yourself with detachment, laugh at yourself perhaps?'

'Oh yes. I always refer to myself as "she". How's "she" looking today? It was worrying sometimes. Although I think there's no woman who doesn't want to look attractive. But it was frightening to be some sort of uncrowned royalty. And to be people's image of themselves.'

The girl who was to become the Princess Di of the movie world was born an unbelievable forty-four years ago in Chicago, the daughter of a Mr Tejaha, a Bolivian engineer immigrant.

'Father was a perfectionist. We had to hop to everything and have marvellous table manners. I could only wear navy blue and grey and white. He wanted me to be interested in tennis and horses just like a little princess, but I couldn't stand such things. I'd seen Laurence Olivier's film of *Hamlet*, and *Red Shoes*, and all I wanted was to be an actress and a dancer.

'I studied Drama at college and I was so uninformed I chose strange audition pieces like Medea. Shakespeare was not a strong suit of mine. American education isn't all it's cracked up to be; they don't respect culture. All they respect is the dollar sign.

'All the same, when I was a child I was a full red, white and blue American. I thought you'd have to commit suicide if you lived in any other country. When I finally got to Europe I thought, My God! What have they been keeping from me all these years?

'When I was eighteen I got pregnant by my high-school sweet-heart, Jim Welch. I must say father was not thrilled. I married Jim and we had two marvellous children, but we weren't compatible. He wanted to go and live in Alaska! Can you see me in an igloo, stripping off blubber and all that stuff?

'We were living in La Jolla, San Diego. It's a fine place if all you want to do is sit and watch a palm tree waving in the air. You know what they say? La Jolla's full of "newly weds and nearly deads and damned old geraniums". I was working as weather girl on television for $7.50 a programme – but I thought, there's another world out there. There's people with bleeding feet throwing themselves down the stairs. There's Betty Grable and Errol Flynn. Jim and I split up after three years. I would have gone to New York but I hadn't got a winter coat and I was afraid of the climate. So I went to Los Angeles.

'My first job in Hollywood, I was a "pin-on" model. They pinned the dresses on me in private. They said my body should never be seen in public. My shoulders were too broad and my hips too slender.

'Then I was a billboard girl on TV for the Hollywood Palace of Varieties. I wore fishnet tights and carried a board advertising next week's programme. Fans started writing in. And then a *Life* photographer, a sort of wholesome version of Helmut Newton, took a lot of photographs of me in the freezing surf in November. He specialized in sportive girls.

'All the time I was finding out how films and television worked. I was always interested in the learning process. I was very shy then really. I didn't say too much. When I got into *The Incredible Journey* with Donald Pleasence [a movie in which Miss Welch went on a submarine trip round a person's arteries] and he talked about all these foreign restaurants, I just couldn't join in with it.

'My second husband was a mail boy when we fell in love. Then he became a producer. He thought he'd mastermind my career. Well, minded it, I suppose – not much of the master. I didn't want that. I do think it hard for a man to be married to a successful woman. A career is erotically sexual; it's my real passion and perhaps I've squandered myself in work. A career is like always having a mistress on the side.'

A change came for Miss Welch when she appeared in Dick Lester's *Three Musketeers*, and was found to have a real comic talent. She has made thirty films, been a huge hit in a Broadway musical and acted with Belmondo in Paris, where she met her present husband, writer, photographer and producer, the Renaissance man who was now into his second plate of oysters.

'The American election? I shan't vote. King Reagan and Queen Nancy, they're just a couple of TV stars and I suppose the option's going to be picked up on their second series. I mean, they've got no style but they're entertaining as hell. American politics is all like Disneyland and if things get dull you can always call in the Marines to recapture the glory of the 1940s, when we were the conquering heroes of the Second World War. I wish they could be honest and say we're just out for our own interests, not protecting democracy when we do awful things in Nicaragua and El Salvador.

'But, anyway, Reagan doesn't really rule America; people we don't know about do that. The Reagans are just fantasy figures. Well, I'm one of those myself. I don't want politicians who just say someone else's dialogue like I do. I mean, I've been inside make-believe all my life and I know the Americans are being sold fantasy. Our politics really are a T V soap, like the Olympic Games.

'About your book . . .'

'Oh, about that?'

'Why do Americans buy so many diet books and jog and talk about their health night and day and they're all so fat? I mean those huge cops you see waddling down the street, so fat they can hardly get at their guns?'

'They eat because they're all anxious. We live in a high-anxiety society. People feel it instinctively, like animals.'

'One more thing . . .'

'Yes?'

'What happened to Jim Welch who wanted to take you to an igloo?'

'Oh, he became a real estate developer. He's very rich.'

Dinner was over. The Renaissance man was going out to spend an hour at Tramps, but Raquel Welch was going for an early night. A good egg, Miss Welch, I thought, and one well able to put up with the considerable disadvantages of being beautiful.

Norman Tebbit in Gaiters?

THE BISHOP OF LONDON

'Why wouldn't Mrs Thatcher make a frightfully good Bishop?'

'That's an excellent question and I'll give you an answer which has nothing whatever to do with whether or not you think Mrs Thatcher is a good Prime Minister. It comes down to the biological difference between men and women. That's why women aren't the right people to be priests.'

Dr Graham Leonard, Bishop of London, Visitor to Europe, Prelate of the Order of Knights Bachelor and Chairman of the Central Religious Advisory Committee, has been called, because of his position in the nation's capital, his voice in the City and the House of Lords, one of the most influential churchmen in the world. He sat in his study, in front of bookshelves full of theology, puffing at his pipe like a rather shy but determined headmaster. Like a headmaster he is very keen on authority and his pronouncements are full of certainty. Not for Leonard of London the tormented gestures of Jenkins of Durham, who will wriggle painfully in his chair, groping for words to describe some elusive and indefinable Godhead. Leonard sits upright and gives it to you as clearly as next term's timetable. Take the Biology of Bishops, for instance; as a former Science student he talks a lot about Biology.

'Biologically man takes the initiative. Woman receives and is feminine.'

At the thought of Mrs Thatcher as a passive recipient the mind boggled for a moment, but Dr Leonard was off into the deeper realms of theology. 'It's not an accident that when God became "man" He chose to be a male. There's no doubt that He could have chosen to be a woman if He'd wanted to. The headship of the Church springs from Christ, so by keeping the priesthood to men we are witnessing to the archetypal headship. You must also remember that He never chose a woman disciple.'

Outside London House, the Bishop's offices and residence, the back streets of Westminster were quiet and deserted. No crowds of outraged feminists were beating at the door. The Movement for the Ordination of Women weren't outside shouting reminders about Mary Magdalene, who accompanied the disciples, and the Woman of Samaria, to whom Jesus gave His message. No infuriated Deaconess was throwing stones at the windows. Dr Leonard fingered his tobacco pouch thoughtfully and made what he clearly felt to be a concession to the opposite sex, although women don't seem to be entirely delighted by it.

'He chose a woman to be the Mother of God. That's the highest role a human being can perform.'

'But looking down on Roman-occupied Bethlehem in the reign of the Emperor Augustus, wouldn't God have been extremely foolish to have sent a woman down to preach about the Kingdom of Heaven? I mean, they didn't take much notice of Jesus; a woman simply wouldn't have had a chance.'

'I think the matter's more fundamental than that.'

'And isn't that why Jesus didn't have a woman disciple? It wouldn't have worked in that society.'

'He broke a lot of other conventions. I've no doubt He would have broken that one if He'd wanted to.'

'But *why* can't women be priests? God created woman in His own image. Surely you would say He created Mrs Thatcher in His own image . . .'

'God created woman in His own image, but in a *different* image. He must contain both sexes . . .'

'And some of the great saints have been women – St Teresa of Avila . . .'

'Saints, yes. But not priests. I think women must accept that being a priest is a role they can't play.'

'So what would you say to all the women who sincerely believe they have a vocation?'

'That they're mistaken.' Dr Leonard had no doubts about it. 'A lot of men sincerely believe they have a vocation to be priests and they're mistaken too.'

'Are you sure God's said His last word on the subject? I mean, society's changed in two thousand years. Mightn't He have had second thoughts?'

'I see no sign of that. I'd want good reasons to believe in a change and the *whole* Church would have to agree. To me the whole matter is decided in the Christian Gospel and the question is whether the Christian Gospel is eternal or subject to social change.'

At the moment 87 per cent of the House of Bishops in the Synod is in favour of the ordination of women, 63 per cent of the House of Laity and 57 per cent of the House of Clergy. But the Church of England, Dr Leonard has said dramatically, 'is like two express trains rushing towards each other down the same track'.

'If the ordination of women is allowed by a majority, would you break away?' I remembered that a couple of months ago a hundred disaffected clergymen met in Oxford to discuss a possible split. The Rector of Cowley said, 'We don't intend to remain in a Church of England that does crazy things like ordaining women.' Dr Leonard was the only Bishop to attend this meeting 'officially'. He said it was wrong to assume that those who objected to women priests would either knuckle under or join other churches.

'It might possibly happen,' the Bishop of London was proceeding cautiously. 'We might have to part amicably with those who ordained women.'

'There could be schism?'

'Yes.'

I thought back to the days of two rival Popes and on to the fascinating prospect of rival Archbishops in London and Canterbury.

'If there was a split in the Church would you consider leading half of it?'

'All I would wish to say' – Dr Leonard was still cautious – 'is that if the situation arose I would be available to do what is right.'

It was not the first time that Dr Leonard has thought that reliable old steam train, the Church of England, was going off the rails. When he was Bishop of Willesden, back in the sixties, he seriously warned, from his Anglo-Catholic position, that a scheme to unite the Anglicans and the Methodists might split the Church.

'Your father was a low church clergyman and you went to Monkton Combe, an evangelical Public School. Why did you change?'

'They had a Christian Union at school. Everyone in it seemed to be saved. I remember that St Paul preached to the Corinthians, among whom were no doubt drunkards and committers of incest. I'm not in favour of that sort of conduct but I think there has to be a Gospel for everyone and there wasn't any message from the Christian Union. And I couldn't say I felt "saved". I just wanted to do something to express my belief.'

Expressing his belief, firmly but not always tactfully, has led Dr Leonard to an ecclesiastical career that might have provided a promising plot for Trollope. In 1978 a newspaper reporter telephoned, as newspaper reporters will, to ask his views on Princess Margaret's friendship with Mr Roddy Llewellyn. Dr Leonard, by then Bishop of Truro, was, as his wife said, 'caught on the hop'. He made some vaguely disapproving noises and added, perhaps unwisely, that 'one of the Princess's options is to back out of public life'. Later he said that he was praying for her, although one churchman took the view that he might have done that more kindly without talking about it. These pronouncements are said to have made Dr Leonard rather less than the Royal Family's favourite

Bishop. He does receive strong support, however, from another quarter. Deprived of the Mitre for reasons of sex Mrs Thatcher is known to be greatly in favour of Dr Leonard's strict call to authority. In 1980, when Canterbury fell vacant, she is said to have preferred Leonard, who was the front-runner, but something, perhaps his unpremeditated remarks to a *Mirror* Group reporter, kept him from the Archbishopric. Runcie, a slow starter, pulled ahead of the field.

In 1981 the See of London became vacant. Dr Runcie was known to favour John Habgood, described as 'a lantern-jawed liberal academic'. The strong body of London Anglo-Catholics supported Leonard but the voting in the Crown Appointments Commission was rumoured to be 7 to 5 in favour of Habgood. However, the Commission sent both names to the Prime Minister as men of equal stature. She chose Leonard's name to send on to the Queen and eventually Dr Habgood found his consolation in the See of York. Mrs Thatcher had got her conservative Bishop installed but she was, perhaps, disappointed if what she had expected was a Norman Tebbit in gaiters. Dr Leonard has voted five times against the Government in the House of Lords, notably on the question of the abolition of the GLC. The Prime Minister still calls for an annual luncheon at London House; history does not relate what she has said most recently to the Bishop.

'Can we discuss miracles?'

Dr Leonard said he would be glad to do so, courteously adding that he was in my hands and indeed had no pressing engagements until dinner-time. His press secretary Norman Hood, a comfortable figure in a soft grey shirt and with a slip of dog collar and a cardigan, passed round tea and biscuits. It may be that he was there, in the gentlest possible way, to field unlooked-for questions about the Royal Family. So we settled down to consider the Resurrection.

'The Bishop of Durham believes that God could have managed

the Resurrection perfectly well if He had wanted to, but that sort of miraculous behaviour is just not in His style. That's how I understand his argument. You think it is just God's style?'

'God's style was to become a man. The second person of the Trinity took human flesh. He had to enter a body. You wouldn't expect that to happen through normal sex, so you get the miracle of the Virgin Birth. That was the point of entry. Now you get the point of departure and I regard the body as very important. It's unthinkable that it wasn't raised up, that it was merely left in the tomb.'

'The Bishop of Durham would also say that concentrating on those sort of miracles puts the ordinary, rational citizen off the Christian religion.'

'Bishops meet a lot of people, Christians and non-Christians. I think they want a Church which says, "This is what I believe. You have to grow into that belief." We have to be clear about what is unmistakably supernatural. The question that divides Christians from non-Christians is "Are we living under judgement?" If you believe that, you must have authority. To undermine authority is to undermine responsibility.'

'Do you think the Church of England is becoming too liberal?'

'Perhaps. In some of its official utterances it seems to be losing its way. There's too little said about sin.'

'What do you think is a sin? Homosexuality?'

'Genital relations between people of the same sex, men or women, is sinful.' The Bishop took a biscuit; he had no doubt on the subject.

'Is sex outside marriage sinful?'

'So far as what you do with your body must affect your soul.'

'So it *is* a sin?'

'Yes.'

Outside the windows anxious clerics in cassocks and anoraks were hurrying into Church House. Westminster Abbey was shrouded in silence. There was one thing you could say for sin, I thought, there's a lot of it about.

'Is divorce a sin?'

'It may not be. It may be a regrettable necessity. But remarriage after divorce is a sin.'

'If your husband or wife ups and leaves you, what are you to do with the rest of your life?'

'I've known cases of husbands and wives coming back, after the death of the other partner.'

It seems that what you are meant to do is wait for a long time. I asked if there wasn't a certain irony in the fact that the Church of England came into being because of a Tudor monarch who wanted to get rid of one wife and marry another with the minimum possible delay.

'Henry VIII was a symptom.' The Bishop smiled tolerantly. 'He wasn't a fundamental to the scriptural authority of the Church.'

'Have you ever had doubts about God?' I asked Dr Leonard, who seemed quite untroubled by this well-known Christian malady.

'At times. Particularly during the war. But it is like living with someone you love. You may not understand what they're doing all the time, but you still go on loving them.'

'The question I can never get answered in these interviews . . .'

'Yes?'

'Is why an omnipotent and loving God allowed the massacre of the Jews, or thousands being drowned in mud in Columbia, or starving in Africa . . .?'

It was a question I had asked a Cardinal and an Archbishop and got nothing but an honest confession of ignorance in the face of divine mysteries. It had caused the Bishop of Durham, almost prone in his armchair, to throw up his feet in bewilderment. The Bishop of London was, once again, free of doubt.

'God is love and love is freedom. He chose to redeem us and

we're free to accept or reject Him. Free will is inevitable in a just world.'

'So the guard in the concentration camp forcing the Jewish family into the gas chamber is free to choose how he behaves?'

'We must all be free. And if you allow freedom to do good, you must have freedom to do evil. It's like the opposite sides of a slope. You can't have one without the other.'

'I can see it's all very nice for the Nazi guard to be free, but looking at it from the point of view of the Jewish family . . .?'

'Just like the opposite sides of a slope. You can't have the slope up without the slope down.'

In its way it was the clearest answer I had had to the question. But I still wondered what great question of freedom arose when children died of leukaemia, or churches full of worshippers were swept away in earthquakes.

'I can't give you a perfect answer to that. If I could I'd be God. But let me say that creation's not static. It's "groaning and travailing in expectation" St Paul said. The physical world can be good or dangerous, and our bodies are full of stress and tension. I would say that suffering and death are not the ultimate evils . . .'

'Do you believe in Heaven?' My time was almost over, the tea was cold in the cups and the Bishop had a dinner to go to.

'It's not simply going to end. There must be eternal life with God.'

'And Hell?'

'The possibility of Hell, yes. I think there must be people incapable of living eternally. They'll eventually become extinct.'

'Would you like to be Archbishop of Canterbury?'

'Oh, I'm too old.' Dr Leonard stood up smiling. 'I'm sixty-four. They wouldn't have me now.'

He showed me out, still smiling, complaining a little at the loss of Fulham Palace, for centuries the spacious home of the Bishops of London, and the difficulties of entertaining in his flat on top of London House where he lives with his wife, Priscilla. 'It's not at all convenient here. We have to park in the street, or in the National Car Park at the end of the road. Very good to see you and talk.' So I left him and Dr Leonard was off, to speak at a dinner, to write another book or his pastoral letter, to rule his huge diocese of London, for which he has the help of no less than five junior Bishops, to make a speech in the House of Lords on Sunday Observance and warn the Church of the dangers of liberal reform. He would delight many Anglo-Catholics, infuriate a large number of women and go about his tasks looking gently amused, confident of the clear authority of the scriptures. When his work was over he would listen to Elgar or Mahler, read T. S. Eliot, or mend things in his workshop. 'I do that,' he said, 'because I'm extremely miserly and against built-in obsolescence.'

This Christmas, as every Christmas, I look forward to Midnight Mass in a village church. No doubt many of the congregation will be sinners according to Dr Leonard's strict definition. Many might not be seriously perturbed if a woman took the service. Some may feel, with Jenkins of Durham, comfort in a spiritual experience which no longer depends on a literal belief in miracles. Others, like Leonard of London, may feel safer under clear religious authority.

Dr Leonard has a good story about a chauffeur who drove him expertly when he was Truro. This admirable man took another Bishop to a remote church which the cleric in question did not think would expect a service in full dress. When the local churchmen seemed disappointed that the Bishop would not appear before them in the glory of his episcopal regalia, the chauffeur came to his master's rescue. 'Don't worry, my Lord,' he whispered, 'I always travel with a spare set in the car.' The Church of England, whatever the future may hold, is still, this Christmas, prepared for the wide variety of demands made upon it. There always seems to be another Mitre in the boot.

The Good Man in the Cast

SIR GERAINT EVANS

'What did you think of your great characters? Falstaff?'

'Full of devilment and gaiety. Rather pathetic. At first I thought of him like Osbert Lancaster, but Osbert's not bald. And then I thought of the big bald head and moustache of Sir Adrian Boult, the fading English gentleman. Also I wanted him to look like a man in our village called Fatty Osborne. I went down to Wales and saw Fatty sitting on a gate. I waited twenty-five minutes for him to get up so I could see him on the move. Then I rehearsed with a rolled-up blanket tied between my legs, so I could walk the way fat men do, you know, with their feet turned out.'

'Don Giovanni?'

'I only played him once. All men want to be Don Giovanni, certainly Falstaff does. And you can feel the women in the stalls all longing to meet the Don. He's looking for perfection and never finds it. Like all of us, I suppose. He feels the grass is greener . . .'

'You've said Figaro stood and faced Count Almaviva like a true revolutionary. Are you a revolutionary?'

'I suppose much less than I was,' said Sir Geraint Evans, son of a coalface worker, sixty-two years old now and about to retire from the operatic stage in a blaze of glory and a sparkling fountain of Donizetti's music. 'But I think Figaro's a good man. An absolutely honest, decent, straightforward character. Really the only one in the opera.'

'Are you a good man?' I asked, and immediately felt guilty, as though the question were calculated to trap the witness into a discreditable admission.

'Yes, I think so,' he answered carefully. 'Yes, I would say I was a good man.'

We had met in the King's Smoking Room at the Royal Opera House, that cosy den under the royal box where our more raffish monarchs are said to have entertained junior members of the *corps de ballet* during operatic *longueurs*.

'Pretty small casting couch,' Geraint Evans said, patting it in passing, and we climbed dark staircases and had a glimpse of dancers rehearsing on the empty stage. 'Freddy Ashton said, "I don't see singers in the wings at dance rehearsals since you left, Geraint." I used to learn ballet steps to help with my acting. Fat men like Falstaff can be very light and nifty on their feet.' And then we arrived at another retiring room behind another box, where we were left alone to have lunch.

'Why does Wales produce such marvellous singers? I mean, is it the rain or something?'

'I think it's the language. We all spoke Welsh at home. It's the open vowels. They have open vowels in the north of England and lots of good singers come from the North Country.' At which point Sir Geraint started to recite 'All through the Night' in Welsh, a caressing, guttural and singing sound which had echoes of Russian and Italian and, when spoken in the vicinity of Pontypridd, leads so naturally to opera that the theatre in Islington used to be called 'Sadler's Welsh'.

'My father was very musical,' Geraint Evans said. 'He conducted oratorios. My mother died when I was very young but she had a lovely mezzo-soprano voice. They both sang regularly in Bethel, the Methodist chapel. My grandmother was blind, so the blind charity gave her a wireless when there were only about three sets in our whole street. I first heard Wagner on Granny's wireless, I sang Elijah in costume at the working men's club when I was seventeen.'

'Do they still do *Elijah* in the working men's club?'

'Dear me, no. Bingo has taken over.'

Once, when there was an accident in the colliery at Cilfynydd, his home village, the boy Geraint, pressing round the pit-head, saw a severed arm fall out of a stretcher. His father was determined he shouldn't work at the coalface and, having a talent for drawing, Geraint Evans became a window-dresser at Mr Theophilus's 'High Class Ladies' Wear' in Pontypridd. When the war started he volunteered for the RAF and ended up singing on the Forces Radio Network in Hamburg. When he was demobbed the kindly Mr Theophilus, who had prospered, offered the young Evans a whole ladies' wear shop of his own, thereby almost robbing the world of a wonderfully shady Leporello and marvellously lecherous old Sir John.

Geraint Evans chose the Guildhall School of Music and progressed, by way of the Nightwatchman in *Die Meistersinger*, to be picked by a percipient Peter Brook to play his first Figaro in the 1949 production at Covent Garden. He was twenty-six years old and earning a princely £20 a week. By that time he had married Brenda, a school teacher who had been born in the same street as the young baritone in Cilfynydd; although Lady Evans, it seems, says that Geraint never proposed to her but simply took their eventual marriage for granted. From then on he seems to have lived a life of great personal happiness and almost uninterrupted professional success.

'When you come on the stage as Figaro and open your mouth for the first time, are you terrified that you won't hit the first note?'

'You know you'll get the first note. That's your job. And you know the part backwards, that's your job also. But it's the support, the strength from here [one hand went to his throat] to here [the other to his groin], that's what you need to keep it going. So you're terrified of any little cold, any draught, any tummy upset, anything that's going to take the strength from you. The only *Rigoletto* I ever did I had a virus and it was terrifying. I could feel the strength collapsing. The voice ended as a sort of croak. But the audience felt it wasn't my fault. They didn't boo me. Do you know, I've never been booed?'

'Do you think booing in the opera house is very cruel?'

'It is cruel. But then applause in the opera is much bigger than in the theatre. The music produces the applause. It's like the cheers at a rugger match at Cardiff Arms Park.

'I always thought the acting was just as important as singing and I've had great directors in opera: Guthrie, Carl Ebert, Peter Brook. Beckmesser in *Meistersinger* is a very pedantic, prissy sort of chap, so I always wore shoes that were too small for me. For Wozzeck, the simple soldier, I wore shoes that were much too big. So far as timing Falstaff goes, I've always modelled myself on Bob Hope and Jack Benny. Claggart, the bullying Master-at-Arms in Ben Britten's *Billy Budd* was played as a stupid Sergeant, but I saw Laughton in *Mutiny on the Bounty*, so I gave Claggart the same walk.' At which moment, with one arm and a leg trailing, Geraint Evans advanced on me in a crab-like manner, smiling and singing, 'What is your name . . .? Able Seaman . . .?' in a voice which filled me with instant terror.

'What do you think about opera in English?'

'Some operas. I think we should do *The Magic Flute* in English because it has so much dialogue. But *Falstaff*! You've got to keep the smell of garlic in the words of the Verdi opera. I mean, which do you like to hear best: 'Honour! Thieves! You are faithful to your honour, you sewers of infamy . . .'' or this?' and he began to sing Falstaff's great aria with all the rancid humour and bitterness of an old man, in a language soaked in garlic. *'L'Onore! Ladri! Voi state ligi all'onor vostro, voi! Cloache d'ignominia . . .'*

The Welsh, I remembered him saying, are short and dark, totally different from the English, closer, perhaps, to the people of the Mediterranean.

*

'In the end the Don defies God and refuses to repent.'

'He does. I think it's just bravado.'

'Do you believe in God?' I asked.

'I do. I don't know about immortality. I think that's the things we can do here, for our children, or charity. The things I try to do for young singers. But my belief in God is very emotional.' He smiled. 'It's very Welsh.'

'What's your favourite opera house in the world?'

'Oh, this, of course.' We had finished our lunch behind the empty box in Covent Garden. 'This is home.'

We went out through the underground passages and the stage-hands and singers all greeted him with great affection. He's a compact, well-dressed man with a sweep of grey hair, who might have been a rugger player or a miner or a window-dresser in Pontypridd, only luckily, the opera got him. Like Figaro, with whom he has lived for the last thirty-six years, he is the good man in the cast. The others still seem unable quite to believe that he will disappear to Wales with his life-long Susanna, to sail his boat out of Abera-eron and sing only to the fish.

Well-known Cemeteries

RUTH RENDELL

When it comes to murder and kindred atrocities there is no doubt that women lead the field. Patricia Highsmith, almost in love with a charmimg and amoral crook, P. D. James, mistress of forensic detail, and Ruth Rendell divide the field. Unlike their predecessors in the Agatha Christie school of detection, their murders are not bloodless crossword puzzles or parlour games to be enjoyed like Dumb Crambo and Consequences. The nature of evil is, for the present generation of women sleuths, a serious business. They not only have the key to the morgue but are not afraid to venture into the criminal's skull.

Perhaps the most startlingly original talent is that of Ruth Rendell, who, after twenty-nine books, is embarking on a second career as Barbara Vine, a more leisurely, detailed but none the less deeply unsettling novelist. This Spring Miss Rendell and Miss Vine will each publish a book, and to meet their combined personalities I set out into the icy regions of East Anglia. The lady waiting for me on Colchester station was dark-haired, good-looking, pale and elegant. She wore patterned black stockings, shining high-heeled shoes and spoke with great precision. Now and again she would laugh quite loudly at some unexpected turn in her life of crime. She bore absolutely no resemblance to Miss Marple.

'Constable country.' As she drove we saw Dedham church tower. 'And Maria Marten's red barn is near our village. Not a very interesting murder really. I thought it was time to move out of North London. I've got to know almost every inch of Hampstead and Highgate.'

'That's what you write about.'

'What I have written. I think you write about what you know, don't you?'

'In your new Ruth Rendell novel *Live Flesh* you write with extraordinary authority about the feelings of a young rapist called Victor. Is his a world you know also?'

At the memory of Victor her laugh came with a burst of unexpected delight. 'I suppose some things depend on the imagination.'

That had been around the time when she [Victor's wife, Pauline] *had begun being more wakeful and active during their sexual moments, wakeful and active to the extent of chatting about what her mother had said to her on the phone that morning and her history tutor's comments on her latest essay. Victor had got up and gone out into the dark and raped a girl who was taking a short cut home through Highgate Wood. The girl had been terrified and had shouted and fought. It wasn't like doing it to a dead sheep with a chit-chat tape playing. It was wonderful.*

I had read Miss Rendell on a criminal's mind and asked about the roots of such behaviour.

'You don't subscribe to the earnest sociologist's view that crime is all a result of a deprived upbringing? Most of your appalling young criminals come from quite comfortable middle-class homes . . .'

'Oh yes. I think it's nature not nurture, don't you? Another thing they're fond of saying is that rape isn't a sex act but "an act of aggression". Victor knows quite well that it's a sexual act.'

'Have you known many criminals?'

'None.'

'Or had any temptation to commit a crime?'

'None. Not even shop-lifting.'

'Then how do you know so much about a rapist?'

'Any woman can imagine what it's like to be raped. I have to get inside Victor's character, to imagine what it's like to have that to contend with. Of course he's terrible but there have to be moments when the reader understands him and even likes him. Writing about the crime is never as important as writing about the character. I have to know the way Victor is thinking.'

'Isn't it depressing, being inside a character like that for nine months, or however long it takes you to write the book?'

'If a depressing thing gives me an idea for a book it ceases to be depressing. The interest overcomes the depression. Criminals are human beings, not monsters, that's what makes them fascinating. Of course it's far easier to write about complicated, difficult, immoral people; but we wouldn't like them in our homes, would we?'

'So writers depend on crime?'

'Oh yes. If crime didn't exist we'd have to invent it.'

We were sitting by the fire in the pink-carpeted drawing-room of a pink farmhouse in the Constable country, drinking white wine. Ruth Rendell's husband Don, a quiet ex-*Daily Mail* journalist, from whom she has been divorced and remarried, was busy doing something about the lunch. Outside, in the big garden where Don grows vegetables, the lawn had been considerably ravaged by moles.

'You have a pronounced taste for the macabre.'

> 'I was not unaware of the flowers and the vines,
> But the hemlock and the cypress
> Overshadowed me night and day . . .'

Miss Rendell quoted Edgar Allan Poe with another healthy laugh. 'I like to remind myself of mortality and all the London cemeteries are well known to me. I enjoy reading things on tombstones, and I like the feeling of decay in Highgate cemetery.'

'Do you frighten yourself when you're writing?'

'Not at all. But I can frighten children and they *love* it. When

141

children come to stay, we sit here in the twilight and I tell them stories about gold prospectors who're eaten by lions, or black scaly things coming out of the lake. They wouldn't enjoy it half as much if the gold prospectors ate the lions. Of course, I'm fond of reading things that frighten me. I love M. R. James's ghost stories, and the most exciting thing I can imagine is to find a hitherto unknown book by Sheridan Le Fanu.'

'Do you believe in ghosts?'

'I think there is something in it. After all' – Miss Rendell laughed again – 'if there were ghosts I'd know about it, wouldn't I?'

Ruth Rendell was born in South Woodford where both her parents were schoolteachers. When she left school she went to work on a group of local papers and Don was put in charge of her. She tried all sorts of writing and wrote six unpublished works, including a light comedy and what she calls 'The Great Jewish Novel', although she is not a Jew. Then she wrote her first Inspector Wexford detective novel and Don helped her to find a publisher, who paid her £75 for it. Now he is delighted by her success, although he finds it impossible to persuade her to take a few days off between books.

'How do you meet anyone like your characters?'

'I walk, I know every inch of great areas of London. I walk about and I watch people. And then I don't just sit about in this pink, ivory tower. I don't just meet the same middle-class friends. I've got to know some strange characters from all the rooming-houses in London. There are quite a lot of them, friends and relatives of people I met in the late sixties. Yes. Some of them are really quite strange.

'A great deal of crime writing isn't about crime. It's about people leading ordinary lives. If you can describe a woman drinking coffee and washing the cup and then cleaning it by running her finger round it – I read that somewhere lately – then the readers recognize it's true and they're with you all the way. Writing isn't a puzzle, but it's about suspense, keeping going with little moments of uncertainty.

'What am I afraid of? I'm afraid of losing my memory, although I'm very healthy and there's no sign of it. I'm scared by the childishness of the heads of Government. And I'm against nuclear weapons. I go to Greenham and I go to Molesworth because I feel it's wrong. I think I've got to do something, even if it's not to any avail. Anyway I enjoy demonstrations. I meet people there. I'm not always pessimistic about human nature, you know, I'm grateful when I see nobility.'

If it weren't for a ridiculous literary snobbery about 'crime writing' Ruth Rendell would be acclaimed as one of our most important novelists. She fearlessly inhabits her own disturbing world, writing incessantly and walking. You may see her any day, walking the streets of London and observing strange people, or enjoying a cemetery, or at an armament base, protesting against some vast organization of death beside which the activities of such as Victor may seem trivial by comparison.

Buzfuz to His Father

PETER NICHOLS

Feeling You're Behind may sound like a state of mild paranoia or a strange way of making advances to yourself. It seemed, I suggested, an unexpected title for a wonderfully funny and courageous autobiography by a man who has had a string of theatrical successes.

'I've always felt I was coming from behind and getting pipped at the post,' Peter Nichols said. 'When I did *Privates on Parade*, about a soldiers' concert party in the Far East, the telly came out with *It Ain't Half Hot, Mum*, which was on the same subject. When we did *Passion Play* in New York we found the title had been used for a novel by Jerzy Kosinski. I was always a late developer. I didn't really get going at all until I was thirty.'

'What happened then?'

'I married Thelma.' He was referring to Mrs Nichols.

'That made all the difference?'

'Regular sex,' he said thoughtfully. 'It allows you to concentrate on other things.'

It's difficult to interview a friend, and I have known Peter Nichols since 1970, when plays we had written about our respective fathers arrived in the theatre at almost exactly the same moment. The interview, taking place fourteen years later, couldn't be a voyage of discovery, but a conversation, postponed for the sake of gossip over a long lunch. And then we were in the sunny top floor of a house in Camden Town with Thelma's paintings and a large vibraphone which Peter Nichols plays along with gramophone records when he is at all worried about catching up, and feels like Lionel Hampton.

'There was so much my father didn't know. He lived in the East End of London for thirty-four years and he didn't know where Mayfair was. Then he came to Bristol and was a traveller for the Co-op. He always seemed old. He was in his forties when I was born and fifty before I got to know him. In a way he was a great puritan. He dreaded drink – his father had been a drunk who knocked him about – and he hated swearing. When I went into the Army the language came as a stomach-churning horror to me. My father was prudish but he believed in natural justice. He was very honest. He never learnt that hypocrisy is needed to get on in life.'

Nichols Senior, who called his son 'Buzfuz', was also a ready-made theatrical character. He had been an amateur Pierrot or smoking-room comedian, and his wardrobe was full of props, a silver-knobbed cane, a vicar's collar and a variety of hats. 'He used to go into every shop in the street and give a performance. He loved it when he'd embark on a long, well-known story and we'd all start laughing at him. He was in his element as the straight man being sent up by the comics.' Whatever his character, Richard Nichols spoke in a music-hall language which was a precious legacy to a playwright son. His umbrella was a brolly or a gamp, his hat was a titfer or a lid, and, 'When I do the charring for cork-tipped Katey [Peter Nichols's mother],' he said, 'I usually run the vacuum along the inside of my trouser turn-ups – gets rid of any scurf, debris, nail-parings, orange peel or general gubbins.'

'John Osborne's grey childhood with a family who always told him that success was not for him made him terribly angry. Was yours like that?'

'Not really. My father went to huge sacrifices to send us to the Grammar School. But no one ever told me anything. All I knew about university, for instance, came from having seen *A Yank at Oxford*.'

'Were there books in the house?'

'Absolutely none. I think the only book my father ever read was *My Cricketing Days* by Don Bradman.'

'But did they expect you to succeed?'

'Not at all. You know what my grandmother said about Ernest Bevin? She said, "They can't make him Foreign Secretary. He's got a Bristol accent." '

With his glasses and somewhat austere features Peter Nichols can look, at first glance, like a schoolmaster, as he once, hilariously, was, or a distinguished writer, a Sean O'Casey or Beckett, photographed for a ponderous article in the *Transatlantic Review*. But his face frequently creases into giggles and he is an excellent mimic, able to give you an instant Harold Pinter with no trouble at all. From sketches in school reviews he went on to act, on one occasion with John Osborne in *See How They Run* at Frinton-on-Sea ('I admired John's acting. It was very cool and full of authority'), and with Albert Finney at Stratford. When he did his National Service he was in Army Entertainment with Kenneth Williams and John Schlesinger. Then he came back to Bristol, the home of other writers, Charles Wood and Tom Stoppard, and a lot of speculation about which of them was feeling most behind.

'You kept very full diaries.'

'I have for a long time.'

'And in your book the quotations from your plays seem interchangeable with the passages of autobiography. I mean, there's really no difference between art and life. Do you ever feel a longing to invent?'

'I think my way of writing came from my father's respect for the truth, or for the facts. Perhaps I sometimes confused truth and facts. I mean, if you push the writing a bit further and invent some of the facts you may come nearer to the truth.

'When I wrote my TV play *Promenade*, Granada took it without any changes because they said they liked the flavour. It had absolutely no moral, no axe to grind. I don't think that would happen now. Morals have been embedded in TV plays by journalists, so *Othello* has to be a play about racial prejudice and battered wives.'

Quite early in their marriage, after a five-day labour, Thelma Nichols gave birth to Abigail, a spastic child who barely reached consciousness in her short life and became Joe Egg, the central character of Peter Nichols's bravest and finest play. The agonized parents joked, made up pantomime dialogue for the inert being they had so painfully produced. They went to hospitals and saw a little boy with a head so huge he couldn't raise it from the pillow, a girl frozen into a sort of permanent crouch.

'How did the whole experience affect you? Did it make you hate God?'

'You mean the manic-depressive rugby footballer in the sky?' Peter Nichols pointed up to the unreliable deity in whom he doesn't believe. 'No. In a way it seemed what I had learned to expect. We had to make jokes about her to keep sane, and to give a character to someone who could never have a character. We found lots of parents doing that. Talking about their "mongrels". I suppose that's what I learnt. The glee in finding that humour clinches a terrible experience.

'We got to hate the hypocrisy of people who felt such children have to be kept alive at all costs. I don't think doctors feel that. No one who hasn't gone through it can possibly understand it. Once Thelma was tempted not to give Abigail the medicine that was keeping her alive, but of course, in the end, she couldn't do it.'

'Do you think that it deepened the relationship between you?'

'I don't think it did any harm. We'd just got married, and we were pushed in at the deep end.'

'What was your happiest time?'

'I suppose it was in the seventies. When we had a house in France. Things were going quite well.'

'And now?'

'The trouble with growing old is that you understand too much. When I was young and went to India to do National Service I was very confused. No one had explained to us that there were several sorts of Indians and they all hated each other. No one told us we were about to give India back to them without any help. And when I saw what all those red spots on the map really depended on . . . Well, I never thought anything like the British Empire could happen again. Lately I've felt very depressed about England, especially since the Falklands War.'

And Peter Nichols has expressed disillusion about the theatre. He's tired of actors who don't want to act and managers who talk only of 'bums on seats' and the incessant temperature-taking worry about 'the business' each week. 'I feel the theatre's a sort of cage really. I used to think its restrictions were invigorating, like having to keep to a strict form in writing a sonnet. But now I feel like writing more freely, without actors and producers getting in the way. The book's a beginning.'

It is not hard, faced with the tragic events of life, to write tragically about them. To express such happenings truthfully in comedy requires talent and courage of a high order, and all the old music-hall jokes Peter Nichols can remember from his father.

Poor Little Rich Girl

GLORIA VANDERBILT

Outside Claridge's Hotel, one sunny September morning, the American tourists were photographing each other beside their hired Rolls-Royces with their arms around their somewhat embarrassed and startled chauffeurs. Inside I was taking breakfast with Miss Gloria Vanderbilt, heiress of the Vanderbilt railway millions, who gave her name to bed-linen, designer jeans, a kind of health food made out of bean curds and christened Tofu, and to probably the most sensational child-custody case to be heard in America in the 1930s. Miss Vanderbilt and I appeared to be of an age, in our early sixties, and from this dizzy promontory I asked for her conclusions about life.

'Life out there?' Miss Vanderbilt spoke with a slight hesitation but clearly, still like a young girl who may sound tentative but knows her own mind. 'I have no illusions about life outside. It's tough. Out there.'

'And inside?' Around us suntanned tourists were ordering breakfast in deep, resonant voices. The waiters padded round us reverently, like undertakers.

'Inside' – Miss Vanderbilt was quite sure – 'inside it's very, *very* romantic.'

So we embarked on the story of her custody case which she has retold, in her book *Once upon a Time*, in the form of a fairy story with herself cast as Snow White surrounded by some quite sinister Beauty Queens and a platoon of dwarf-like lawyers.

'You were a very rich little girl. I mean, you inherited four million dollars when you were two. The rich are meant to be different from us. Did you feel different?'

'I think you take the world you're born in for granted. I couldn't think of any other world.'

'Did you ever see poor people?'

'Once an old woman opened the door of my Aunt Gertrude's Rolls and tried to sell us apples. She wanted us to do something for her.'

'How did you feel about that?'

'Terrified.'

'What was your world?'

'A caravan. Travelling round hotels in Europe in a Hispano Suiza with my grandmother Morgan and Dodo, the nanny whom I called "Big Elephant", and a beautiful, elusive, fleeting mother who wasn't there as often as not. After all Mother was only twenty when my father died. I can understand that she wanted a good time and her idea of *that* was to be in Europe where her beautiful, identical twin sister, Lady Furness . . .'

'Was having an affair with the Prince of Wales?'

'Well, yes. He was always very nice when we saw him, very polite.'

'The allegation made in the custody case was that your mother was living on your money, really that she wanted you with her to pay the hotel bills in Europe.'

'I suppose she used my money. That was very appropriate. I mean, I had money and she was looking after me. Of course I spent most of my time with grandmother Morgan and the Big Elephant.'

'Your grandmother Morgan was your mother's mother?'

'Yes.'

'And yet in the case she gave evidence against your mother. She turned against her own daughter completely.'

'It was Germany that did it, I think. My mother seemed to be about to marry Prince Hohenlohe and grandmother Morgan had an obsession about me being taken away to Germany. I think she became a little unbalanced. She wanted me to stay in America and be the heiress to the whole Vanderbilt–Whitney empire. She was very ambitious for me about that.'

The battle for Gloria Vanderbilt burst over the child's head when she was nine years old. The Vanderbilts were represented by the strange Aunt Gertrude Whitney Vanderbilt, who wore trousers when it was unusual for women to do so and was frequently topped by a man's Fedora hat. Aunt Gertrude had a number of lovely homes, including a 'Renaissance Palace' on Fifth Avenue, a 'Venetian Palace' on Long Island and a 'mansion with a race course and 2,000 acres of hunting land' in South Carolina. Ably abetted by grandmother Morgan, this formidable lady, who financed the Whitney Museum of Modern Art, launched proceedings for Gloria's custody which became the daily front-page news of the entire American press.

'Part of the evidence was given "behind closed doors". You can imagine what a sensation that caused.'

'Did you ever discover what that evidence was?'

'In a very brutal way. A girl at school told me. One of the boys had been expelled for homosexuality and she said, "You should understand about that because your mother's a lesbian." They suggested mother'd had an affair with Lady Milford Haven.'

'Did the Judge believe that?'

'I think it influenced him, when he gave me to Aunt Gertrude.' To Aunt Gertrude, I thought wonderingly, who wore a Fedora hat and was said to have fallen passionately in love with the daughter of the Vanderbilt architect. Not for the first time in my life I agreed that child-custody cases had all the nightmare qualities of a Grimms' fairy tale.

'But you gave evidence against your mother. You told the Judge you only wanted to live with your Aunt Gertrude.'

'Yes.'

'And you were lying?'

'Oh, yes.'

There is a photograph of the nine-year-old Gloria – a solid-looking child with the same dark, shiny, shoe-button eyes that she has today, and the same look of demure determination – arriving at the New York courthouse with a cape and a small feather in her pudding-basin hat. There she braved the exploding flash bulbs and the shouts of the reporters and a crowd who were all her mother's supporters and against the rich Vanderbilts. Once inside the Judge's chambers little Gloria administered the final blow to her mother's hopes for custody.

'Why did you do that?'

'The lawyers told me that if I didn't stay with Aunt Gertrude I'd be parted from my nanny. She was a big fat lady, German, and she'd been married at sixteen to a man called Ernest Ball who wrote "When Irish Eyes are Smiling". She didn't like Mr Ball very much but she was an ideal mother. I'd've said anything not to be parted from my nanny. I was terrified of losing her.'

'And when the case was over the Judge ordered Nanny Dodo to leave you?'

'Yes. He said she'd turned me against my mother.'

'So they all betrayed you. What did that do to your faith in human nature?'

'I hate anything at all that looks like self-pity. I just became very, very angry.'

'Later on you saw quite a lot of your mother . . .'

'Oh yes. I was allowed to see her at weekends and for a month in the summer.'

'Did you ever tell her why you'd told lies in court?'

'Oh no. We never talked about that. My mother never talked about it at all. We got on very well. But no one ever talked to me about the case. I wish I had talked to my mother about it, before she died.'

'When did you finally feel released from this sort of nightmare childhood?'

'When I was about fifteen, when I discovered I was attractive. I had to get married to get away from Aunt Gertrude, who always wanted me to go out with a chaperon when none of my friends did. So I married my first husband when I was seventeen. It was a great mistake. I should have married Howard Hughes. I was in love with him and I was incurably romantic, as I still am. My first marriage lasted three years. Then I married the conductor Leopold Stokowski when I was twenty-one.'

'How old was he?'

'I don't know, I never asked him. We parted after ten years and I'd had two children. He said he'd put me through a custody case which would make "In the Matter of Vanderbilt" look like a picnic. In the end all he could allege against me was that, because I was an actress at the time, I didn't get up until 10 a.m. But I loved Stokowski, I felt protected by him and I trusted him. Then I married Sydney Lumet the film director.' Miss Vanderbilt's last husband, the writer Wyatt Cooper, died after a happy marriage during which she had two sons of whom she is extremely proud.

'And so you went into business. Jeans and perfume and bean curds . . .'

'I market things. I design the packaging.'

'And give them your name.'

'Yes.'

'Why do you bother to do that? It can't be the money.'

'The only money that means anything to me is the money I make myself.'

'Do you ever feel guilty? About the enormous difference between rich and poor, for instance . . .'

'I'm not really a political person. I'm greatly in favour of free enterprise.'

'And President Reagan?'

'Oh yes. I'm a hundred per cent behind *him*.'

'If you'd been a poor little girl and still been fought over in a violent custody case, do you think your life would have been very different?'

'I can't tell that. How can I tell?'

'You were brought up to be a Catholic. Do you believe in an afterlife?'

'Oh yes. I believe in that.'

'So do you think you may meet them all again? Aunt Gertrude and your mother and Lady Furness and Prince Hohenlohe and the Prince of Wales and the Big Elephant? Will they all be there?'

'Oh yes. I think I may meet them.' Miss Vanderbilt smiled. 'But I hope under happier circumstances.'

'From the photographs in your book you look like a resilient child. Quite tough . . .'

'Not "tough" '. The word was clearly unromantic. 'I prefer the word "resilient". I chose to write the book as a sort of fairy story when someone in the family sent me a photograph of myself as a little girl. I knew the book had to be written as the little girl saw it.'

'Do you think she really saw it as a fairy story?'

'I don't know. I can't be sure. It was all a long time ago.'

So Miss Gloria Vanderbilt went off to have her photograph taken and I thought how resilient, not to say tough, children are. I thought of all the children who have survived the awful custody cases I used to do as a lawyer, proceedings which grown-ups only use to hurt and wound each other. Children can survive many misfortunes: poverty, neglect, custody cases and even, it seems, inheriting four million dollars at the age of two.

The Man from the Ministry

SIR FRANK COOPER

'If you could wave a wand and deprive Russia of all nuclear weapons, do you think the world would become a safer place?'

'No – much more dangerous.'

I blinked. There I was in the upper reaches of the Ministry of Defence, sitting on a sofa opposite Sir Frank Cooper, the Permanent Under-Secretary, warily sipping a cup of MoD coffee, which he had warned me was particularly foul. I was in the very heart, the nerve-centre, of the pro-Bomb establishment, and the cheerful man opposite me warmly welcomed the possession of such deadly weapons by the power that we are constantly being told is threatening our very existence.

'Could you explain that?'

'Yes, of course.' Sir Frank smiled patiently. 'It's very important that Europe has a strong Nato Alliance and a strong Warsaw Pact. That's what leads to stability. We need to understand that, if we're to avoid a catastrophe, Russia has to feel secure. Remember what terrible losses she suffered during the last war. She has to feel safe from attack. Both sides have to feel safe, and East and West have to go on talking.'

'But there's nothing to show that the West's piling up of more weapons makes Russia more willing to talk. Isn't the proliferation of weapons simply increasing the danger of a "catastrophe", as you call it?'

'There is that danger, yes.'

'What do we do about it?'

'We must be aware.' Sir Frank looked distinctly aware. 'And we must talk to the Russians . . .'

'Do you do that? I mean, do you have any contact with your opposite number in the Russian Ministry of Defence?' I had a vision of two comfortable middle-aged men sipping vodka in some neutral atmosphere and agreeing about many things, including their countries' need to sit, for reassurance, on an ever-growing stockpile of engines of mutual annihilation.

'We used to do that. We used to exchange visits to staff colleges and so on. I think it was very useful. We can't really do it now.'

'Why not?'

'Blotted copy-books,' said Sir Frank firmly.

'Oh?'

'Afghanistan and Poland. The Russians have blotted their copy-books there.'

'Yes. Of course.'

'You know, people go on and on about nuclear war; millions and millions of people died in the 1914 War, it just took longer to kill them, that's all.'

Sir Frank smiled at me as I faced up to the coffee. He seemed to derive some comfort from the thought.

Frank Cooper was born sixty years ago, the son of an area manager for Terry's chocolate, and he still thinks of himself as a Manchester radical and a provincial. He went to Pembroke College, Oxford, after Manchester Grammar School and was articled to a firm of chartered accountants. Then the war came and he served as a pilot. 'Merlyn Rees was the fitter who repaired Frank's Spitfire during the war,' someone said when Rees held the Northern Ireland Office and Cooper was his Permanent Under-Secretary, 'and their relationship is the same today.'

When he came home from the war, Frank Cooper rejected accountancy as being too dull, and took up life as a civil servant.

I suggested that many people might not think of that as the most glamorous of careers.

'They'd be wrong. I've found it enormously stimulating. I suppose if you were stuck in the bowels of the Department of the Environment . . . But I've always been interested in Defence.'

'Is it all like *Yes, Minister*? Are you really in control?'

'No,' Sir Frank explained carefully, 'I run the business side of the enterprise. Let's say, I've never had bad relations with any Minister.'

'What would happen if there were a Labour Government who wanted to abandon all our nuclear weapons and forbid Cruise missiles?'

'Well.' The Permanent Under-Secretary smiled. He is a small-ish, bullet-shaped man with a gentle, almost lisping voice, who looks perpetually amused. 'There's always the generals to consider.'

'I expect there are . . .'

'No doubt there'd be a right old row.'

'No doubt there would. But in the end . . .?'

'In the end, if the electors voted for it, we'd have to do it. No doubt about that.'

Remembering the cries of horror that greeted Mr Ken Livingstone's recent invitation to a chat extended to Sinn Fein leaders, I asked Sir Frank about the period when the Government itself was busily setting up talks with members of the same organization. In the mid-seventies there were negotiations over a ceasefire, and conversations were organized by top civil servants with Sir Frank standing firmly in the shadows.

'Did you talk to the Sinn Fein yourself?'

'No, but I organized the people who talked.'

'Would you say it was a secret if I asked you who those people were?'

'Yes, I'd say it was a secret. The object was to get rid of internment and bring back the rule of law.'

'Can you see any solution in Northern Ireland?'

'Not for a long time. The British and the Loyalists in Northern Ireland have never understood each other. They feel intensely British, and yet they're totally different from us. They believe they're independent, and yet they want to be part of Britain. It comes of having had a provincial legislature. Dangerous things, those.'

Ken Livingstone's error in following in the footsteps of Government Ministers and Sir Frank Cooper lay, no doubt, I thought, in having tried to do the thing in public. A quiet cup of tea in Mr Livingstone's bed-sit, with only the newts as witnesses, might have been more in line with the way we order things in Government.

But it was time to move on to our allegedly finest hour. In 1976, Sir Frank moved to the Ministry of Defence and six years later found us unexpectedly at war.

'I was amazed at the public reaction to the Falklands War,' he said. 'I mean, I remember Suez and I expected at least a certain amount of opposition.'

'What was the reason for the war's extraordinary popularity?'

'I suppose we won and everyone likes a winner. Then it was a rather simple issue, if you believe in democracy, which actually I'm not sure many people do in the world today . . .'

'There's been a lot of criticism about the way you handled the news from the Falklands.'

'I don't think we'd done enough preparation on that and we were certainly slow in getting film back. I think the rule was that we didn't mislead people: but we didn't give the full details. If I'd said, "Our chaps will land on the Falklands tomorrow," I'd've deserved to be left alone with a pistol in the top drawer and relied on to do the decent thing.'

'What you said was that there'd be no D-Day-type invasion. The next day the troops went ashore in force.'

'Well, that was strictly true. The D-Day landing was against opposition, on occupied beaches, with a large number of casualties. We weren't going to have one of those.'

'I see.' Or, rather, I thought I saw, the subtle distinction evolved by the ingenious Permanent Under-Secretary. 'You also never denied press reports that the nuclear-powered submarine *Superb* was in the South Atlantic. It was never there in fact?'

'No, it never was. Those reports were very helpful to us.'

I remembered what Sir Frank had told a member of the House of Commons Defence Committee who had questioned him: 'You, as a politician, know as well as anyone that news is handled by anybody in politics in a way that redounds to their advantage.'

'Coming to more recent events,' I said, 'why did this Government seem to deny that an American defence headquarters was to be built near High Wycombe and now it's admitted?'

'The Government got in a muddle about that, as Governments do from time to time,' Sir Frank said cheerfully. 'It's a fall-back headquarters. The Russians have got lots of them all over the place. They're all holes in the ground, you know,' he added kindly, as though trying to cheer me up.

'If you believe that the whole truth shouldn't necessarily be told in time of war, would you also apply that to other topics? I mean, it might be very expedient for a Government not to tell the whole truth about our economic situation, for instance, or not to contradict rumours which might help the pound.'

'On the whole I'm in favour of open Government,' said Sir Frank, as though that, after all, were that.

'Then let me ask you about spies.'

'Oh yes.' The atmosphere lightened considerably. 'The English love spies, don't they? You've only got to go and look at a W. H. Smith's bookstall to see how much we love them. John Buchan's *Greenmantle*. All that sort of thing.'

'I mean, do spies really represent any sort of danger, outside of television serials? Would it make the slightest difference if all our military secrets were published on the front page of the *Daily Telegraph*?'

'It would let the Russians know what kind of weapons we were developing, and they could work out the defences to them.'

'But, if you agree that the purpose of all these weapons is only to be used as a kind of bluff, I mean a kind of balance of terror, then why not broadcast exactly what we've got?'

'We do a certain amount of that anyway. But there are other sorts of secrets, diplomatic secrets . . . that sort of thing.'

Sir Frank seemed anxious not to lose the Great British Spy Hero too easily, although he agreed that spying, like our other great national interests, cricket and murder, had gone down-market. 'We seem low on ideological spies at the moment,' he said. 'Nowadays they do it for money and sex, in rather small quantities.'

'What will you do when you retire?' It had been rumoured that Sir Frank might join Mrs Thatcher's office, but the job eluded him.

'Well, I won't plant turnips. I'll do something. And I'll read the novels I haven't had time to read. Trollope, for instance, and go on listening to music . . . Beethoven, Brahms, Mahler. Running this place has been like running an enormous business. I'm proud of having reduced the staff by about 55,000, and coming in at £5 million under our £12-billion budget. I think we've done quite well. Now someone else can take it over.'

Before I left, I asked Sir Frank what he thought of the ladies of Greenham Common.

'Of course they're very sincere. But I think they're dangerous. As I said, both sides have got to feel strong, and secure. Also, as I say, they forget about the millions killed in conventional wars.'

'You mean we should also be trying to limit conventional weapons?'

'I think so.'

'But aren't you selling them?'

Sir Frank looked at me politely and I began to feel that I was in some way naive in referring to the MoD's wholly owned subsidiary International Military Services Ltd, which supplies assorted weaponry to an eager world market.

'Should you be doing that?' I asked.

'I hope we only sell to friendly countries, and not to upset the balance of power. But the world being what it is . . . if we didn't do it, someone else would.'

Sir Frank waited patiently for the next question. He seemed, on the whole, to be a man born without doubt and is, as he has said, a natural optimist. I tried to grope for some of his optimism and said, at last, 'I suppose America and Russia have got no logical reason to go to war about anything.'

'Yes. But wars don't start for logical reasons, do they? Who can remember a logical reason for the 1914 war?'

I drove to my home, perilously close to High Wycombe, where the Americans were about to be inserted into holes in the ground. Out of all these sincere people, I wondered, who had the best guess – the disarmer of Greenham or the retiring Permanent Under-Secretary listening to Mahler in his Chislehurst home with his cheerful faith in the security of our escalating balance of terror?

Only a few things, I thought, were sure: the Ministry of Defence will continue to be run like an enormous business, and the protesters will protest, and Governments will get into a muddle as Governments always do. For exactly how long, of course, remains another question.

The Meaningful Musical

HAL PRINCE

'Today, when something is not worth saying they sing it,' wrote Beaumarchais in *The Barber of Seville*. To which might be replied that if something is important, heartfelt and passionate enough to be sung, it should be sung as well as the human voice can manage it, by Domingo or Pavarotti or Kiri Te Kanawa; it should burst forth to the music of Mozart or Verdi, to the words of Boito or Da Ponte; and it should not be rustily intoned by a stage actor, or set to music which hovers in a nondescript fashion between the palm court and the top of the pops.

In the deeply truthful world of opera everything is believable, from inviting a statue to dinner to carrying your dead daughter around in a sack. In the make-believe world of the musical the jollity too often seems desperately forced and I have never been able to watch a collection of straw-hatted, dungareed chorus boys prancing about the stage with pitchforks and singing, 'Oh What a Beautiful Morning!' without embarrassment. Worse, perhaps, are the musical's moments of emotion: the song 'When You Walk through a Storm' in *Carousel* being, to me, Broadway's answer to 'Christopher Robin is Saying His Prayers'. When it was suggested that the latest, no doubt extremely talented, composer of musicals is the reincarnation of Puccini, I immediately felt that we should all do better to save up for the next revival of *Tosca*.

So it was as no dedicated devotee of the American Musical that I set out to meet its driving force and inspiration, its impresario, director and most bewitching creator of stage pictures, and the man entitled to put its case with the greatest conviction.

It was a June day in 1980 when I drove to Drury Lane theatre where Mr Hal Prince had, said the Press Office, an 'availability' in the morning. The Stephen Sondheim–Hal Prince musical *Sweeney Todd* was due to open there in a few days' time.

The show came with claims to a large significance. As I drove up to London on the motorway, there was the light and pleasing voice of Mr Hal Prince chatting on the radio. 'The hero is Sweeney the Murderer,' he said. 'It's the source of Greek Tragedy . . . There the victims are motivated . . . Sweeney Todd is the victim of the class system . . .' At which, the Rabbi who was also on the programme agreed that musicals such as *West Side Story* do in fact provide 'wonderful pulpit stuff'.

'Hal' – Mr Stephen Sondheim's voice murmured gently along the motorway – 'is very socially and politically minded. He saw the social problems in *A Little Night Music*.'

'Sweeney Todd,' said Mr Prince, 'is about the dehumanization of the human spirit and the need for revenge.'

Half an hour later I was sitting in the empty auditorium at Drury Lane, looking at the set. To emphasize the dehumanizing influence of the Industrial Revolution, Hal Prince bought a derelict scrap metal factory in Rhode Island and re-erected it on stage.

The huge, rusty building, the great pipes and gables and scaffolding tower up to the Theatre Royal's painted ceiling and demonstrate what has long been known to *Vogue* photographers: that there is nothing more elegant than industrial debris.

The relics of the previous night's rehearsal, which had lasted until eleven o'clock, littered the stalls: empty plastic beakers, tins of cigarette stubs and an old paper bag of half-eaten sandwiches on the lighting table. As I sat alone and waiting, I picked up a script and read one of the lyrics in which Mr Sondheim expresses the effect of the Industrial Revolution on man:

> There's a hole in the world
> Like a great black pit
> And it's filled with people
> Who are filled with shit
> And the vermin of the world
> Inhabit it . . .

As Beaumarchais said, it may all sound better sung.

Then two huge clusters of ceiling lights came on and the old glass factory roof was lit very beautifully and would, no doubt, look magical on the night. It was then I discovered that I was waiting in vain for Mr Prince at Drury Lane, as he was waiting for me in the Savoy Hotel.

'Don't apologize. Please don't apologize. Come up to the room and just relax.'

Mr Prince was standing in the lobby, a small man who looked much younger than his silvery hair and trim grey beard. His eyes shone brightly, he wore his spectacles on the dome of his suntanned forehead, and he smiled with considerable charm.

Dressed in clean jeans and a neat zipper jacket, swathed in some agreeable toilet preparation, he had the air of twinkling, gnome-like impertinence of a Rumpelstiltskin who would guarantee to weave the dullest straw into a golden smash hit before the night is out.

'About me. You want to talk about me?' Mr Prince had steered me out of the empty sitting-room of his suite to a corner of the bedroom. He sat on an upright chair at the dressing-table mirror, toying with what I think was the tape of a letter he was longing to send off. He looked frequently at his watch, and as often at the clock on the wall. He has, an actor who has often worked with him had told me, an extremely low threshold of boredom. He will think up a moment of wonderful theatricality and then have to flee the theatre to avoid the tedium of seeing it rehearsed over and over again.

'Well. You know. Who your father was. That sort of thing.'

'New Yorker. Upper middle class. A stockbroker who voted Republican. There wasn't much religion, we were old German Jews. Very enlightened. But we went to the theatre a lot. A regular ceremony. Saturday afternoons. I saw everything. Orson Welles in the Mercury Theatre, and then Lorette Taylor in *The Glass Menagerie* . . . Opera? My grandmother took me to opera.'

'I don't know about this,' I said, 'but I had a toy theatre . . .'

'Oh, sure. I did too.' Mr Prince smiles. 'I guess it's always the same route.

'At the weekends I did operas in my puppet theatre. That was when they broadcast them over the radio. I went to College. University of Pennsylvania, nothing too grand. I wrote a lot of shows. Then I got conscripted.'

'Any particular war?'

'What was called the Korean Conflict. You know, my family came over from Germany a long, long time ago. They were Rubins and Steins and Mandelbaums. I don't think they were running away from any sort of pogrom. They came to avoid conscription. And they were entirely justified.'

'Did you actually have to visit Korea?'

'Not at all. In our country the Army has this system. They only send the poor, the black and the illiterate out to do the actual fighting. But I got to see Paris and Rome and London. I was very grateful for it.'

'And the theatre?'

'I wrote to George Abbott, the most prolific director–manager. He's ninety-four now. I wrote to him and said, "I can't imagine what I could do for you that'd be worth 10 cents so I'll work for you for nothing. But from the way I do my work you'll never be able to guess that you're not paying me." ' Mr Prince smiled, justifiably pleased at the brilliance of this letter which had got him his first job as an assistant stage manager with the great Abbott.

'I was an ASM for a while. Then I became a second stage

manager. Then we managed to put together our own show, *Pajama Game*.'

'Is that the one with "Take him, pajamas look great on him"?'

'No. It's the one with "Steam Heat" and "Hernando's Hide-Away" and "Hey there, you with the stars in your eyes".'

'And it was a huge hit?'

'And how! We used all sorts of people no one had used before, like Bob Fosse to do the choreography. *Pajama Game* had a social content. It was about labour unrest in a pyjama factory. But I guess the social content was pretty well concealed.'

'And then?'

'Well. We went on having hits . . . *Damn Yankees*, *West Side Story*.'

Hal Prince met Stephen Sondheim in the aisle at a performance of *South Pacific* in 1949. Sondheim was then nineteen and was being taken out by the Hammersteins; Prince was twenty-one and was the guest of the Rodgers. No one dreamed at that meeting that the two young men would become the successors to their elder escorts, and take the healthy sailors of *South Pacific* all the way from the slums of West Side New York to the dubious meatpie shops of Victorian London. Sondheim brought *West Side Story* to Prince to produce, and it seems that when Bernstein played the music, Prince sang, and Bernstein said 'My God, he's so musical. A musical producer!'

After *West Side Story* and *A Funny Thing Happened on the Way to the Forum*, Sondheim and Prince struck a more serious note with *Company*. Prince has said he envisaged a show 'which could examine attitudes towards marriage, the influence upon it of life in the city, and collateral problems of special interest to those of us then in our forties'. If a new way of writing musical comedies had not been discovered, at least there was a new way of talking about them.

'I owe a great deal of my politicalization to my wife,' said Mr Prince, taking another furtive look at the clock. 'I married Judith in 1961. Her step-father had been turned out of California in the McCarthy era, and she was very responsible. I wasn't responsible until I met her. I just thought, Truman dropped the Bomb and well, that's it. Now, I suppose I'm a confused liberal.'

'As a confused liberal, what do you say to those people who accuse you of glorifying a Fascist, Madam Peron in the musical *Evita*?'

'I say they're dim-wits. Look. The Che Guevara character tells them. Argentina was Number Two in gold in the world! The Perons got rid of the gold. It was top in meat. They lost the meat. We actually show thugs beating people up.'

'But what are we meant to feel about her?'

'Ambiguous. Some good. If she stole half of what they say, she still gave half of it away. But she was corrupted by power. We should feel ambiguous.'

'But you use stage magic to excite the audience in exactly the same way the Nazis did.' I remembered the feeling that I had on the first night of *Evita*, that I was watching the biggest hit since the Nuremberg Rally.

'Oh, sure. I took the whole set from the Nazis. The long black banners and all that. I wanted to manipulate the audience, with the Nuremberg techniques. That way they'd understand the feelings of Fascist enthusiasm. I don't agree with any kind of Brechtian alienation.'

A question hung in the air, and I was left wondering when the audience was meant to become alienated from *Evita*, if ever. And then I wondered how alienated they would be at another ballad of degradation, Stephen Sondheim's cheerful number in honour of human pies.

> 'What is that?'
> 'It's a Priest. Have a little Priest?'
> 'Is it really good?'
> 'Sir, it's too good,

> At least.
> Then again, they don't commit sins of
> the flesh,
> So it's pretty fresh.'
> 'Awful lot of fat.'
> 'Only where it sat.'

'It's sensational-horror, Grand Guignol,' Mr Prince said. 'You have Grand Guignol over here. It's just about unknown in America.'

My stricture of musicals for not being operas was met by Hal Prince equally reasonably. He was about to direct Puccini's *Turandot* at the Vienna State Opera.

'As Steve says . . . There was a kind of split between Grand Opera and Light Opera. Grand Opera went on to a sort of lofty plane; but musicals and Light Opera should be of equal status. You're quite happy to do *Die Fledermaus* at Covent Garden at Christmas; why shouldn't you do *Carousel*?'

I wondered why not indeed, and came to the conclusion that at least in *Die Fledermaus* no one has to Walk through a Storm with Their Head Held High. I also wondered about the voices.

'Some singers only get a reputation because they sing in opera houses. We've got a girl who plays Johanna in *Sweeney Todd*. She's sung in opera.'

'But musical music is neither one thing nor the other. It's not classical or pop. It's just show music.'

'It can't be pop while pop is rock.'

'No one goes around whistling tunes out of musicals any more.'

'They whistle "Don't Cry for Me Argentina". But a pop song has to be something that belongs to a singer, so it can either be sung by a girl or a feller. A song in a musical has to belong to a character.'

'Are you always going to work in the musical theatre?'

'I hope not. But when I do a play it has to be something like Dürrenmatt's *The Visit*.'

'A spectacular piece. So you could do Shakespeare?'

'I guess I could. But I love Chekhov. And I should be wrong casting for Chekhov.'

'How do you feel about death?'

'Not much. I keep going.' Mr Prince looked at his watch and at the clock on the wall in rapid succession. 'I suppose I live for the moment. I'm not nostalgic, I don't look back with pleasure at the past. If I did it might make things more comfortable for those who live around me.'

'And God?'

'I can see myself becoming more interested in religion in time. In the metaphysics of religion. I don't care for all the stagey side of church-going.'

'Not with your theatrical talent? I should have thought you would.'

'Oh no. I guess I can always see round to the back of the scenery, and to the unpainted canvas and the batten with the name of the play scrawled on it.'

A Reluctant Joan of Arc

KATHARINE GRAHAM

'I was out on my farm in Virginia and my Editor at the *Post* came out and said there had been two rather strange stories which seemed to him of about equal and transient appeal. One was about a car which crashed through the wall of a house, disturbed two people in an amorous position on the sofa and came out the other side. The other was the fact that some burglars in surgical gloves had been caught in the Democratic headquarters.'

So Mrs Katharine Graham, proprietor of the *Washington Post*, first heard of the Watergate scandal which led her to become the heroine, almost the well-heeled Joan of Arc, of the American liberal establishment.

'As a matter of fact, I'm not particularly liberal. Read our editorials and you'll discover the paper's not really liberal, either. Reagan? A very smart politician. He always was.'

The heavy 90-degree summer heat had settled over Washington, slowing the tourists, who climbed like flies up the white marble steps to see President Lincoln, sitting in his stone chair, look down on them with an ironic grin.

The day before, as a marine band played 'Ruffles and Flourishes', I had heard Ronald Reagan, in a lightweight suit and Californian tan, tell a congress of lawyers, with unrelieved cheerfulness, that America faced a deadly conspiracy of terrorists backed by Iran, North Korea, Libya, Cuba and Nicaragua. Those countries, he had said, drawing a metaphor from old Bugs Bunny cartoons, were ruled by 'misfits and looneytunes'.

Something would be done about these enemies, the President assured us as we sat beneath the huge star-spangled banner that fluttered from the ceiling. It would be done by him and the American people, and would have to be seriously thought about by the American Bar Association.

What it was, was not entirely clear; but it would no doubt be the terror of the earth. Sitting amongst the lawyers, it had occurred to me that the President was about to use the unlikely occasion to declare war on Nicaragua. 'No, he won't do that,' said Mrs Graham. 'The country wouldn't tolerate it. He talks in that way because he's got a right-wing constituency to satisfy. He's a very smart politician and he's very pragmatic.'

The proprietor's office at the top of the *Washington Post* building seemed far removed from the bands and plastic lapel labels and standing ovation of the lawyers' convention. Mrs Graham, immaculate in a blue dress, a tall, good-looking, grey-haired woman of sixty-eight, adjusted a small but ornate tape recorder – an instrument which looked something like a powder compact – and began the unconcealed bugging of our conversation.

She had been born to wealth and to inherit the paper. 'My father, Eugene Meyer, was a Republican Conservative and my mother had terrible rows with Mrs Roosevelt. I suppose we lived in a big house in Washington – it stretched for about half a block. My father was a stockbroker, but he always wanted a newspaper. It was his idea of public service.

'When he bought the *Washington Post*, he did what I've always tried to do, appoint an Editor with whom he was in general agreement and then let him be more or less independent. My mother knew a lot of eggheads; people like Thomas Mann came to visit.' Mrs Agnes Meyer, known as 'Big Ag' and a Washington legend, was also a tireless worker for the public good, much interested in birth control and education.

Katharine Meyer was educated at Vassar and Chicago University, from which she emerged in 1938 as a dedicated New Dealer, and went to work on the *San Francisco News*.

'You were quoted in *The Times* as saying you were "the youngest and silliest girl reporter on the paper". What did you do silly?'

'Silly?' Mrs Graham smiled sometimes and with a shy charm, but not on this occasion. 'I don't think I did anything silly. I covered labour stories. I got pretty well known on the waterfront.'

'Yes, of course.' I moved hastily away from the allegation of youthful silliness. Katharine Meyer had married Philip Graham at the age of twenty-three. 'My husband was a young New Dealer. He had been a law clerk to Mr Justice Frankfurter, who came to sit on the Supreme Court.'

Eugene Meyer turned the company over to Philip Graham in 1947, and Katharine stayed at home to bring up four children. Mr Graham suffered tragically from manic depression and finally shot himself. At the age of forty-six Katharine Graham became President of the Washington Post Co. and now controls *Newsweek* and radio and television stations as far away as Florida and Detroit. She has interests in paper mills, a news service and the *International Herald Tribune*.

Such was her empire when men with rubber gloves were found in Washington's Watergate Building, and the *Post* began the long period of investigation and the painful uncovering of truth which destroyed President Nixon.

'Did you ever feel sorry for him?'

'I suppose I felt sorry for him when he resigned. As a matter of fact, I don't like fights. I always worry about the other side. But they were being so tough with us, attacking us every day, saying we were trying to prove guilt by association.'

Not only that, I remember that the Attorney-General, John Mitchell, had said with his customary delicacy that Mrs Graham 'had got her tits caught in the mangle'. Apart from the abuse, there was a real possibility of losing her licence to run her television stations, if the *Post* had been indicted for a criminal offence after publishing the 'Pentagon Papers'.

'Did you ever have doubts during that time?'

'Of course. Sometimes I thought we were being set up, and someone was feeding us misleading information in order to trap us. But Ben Bradlee, our Editor, told me everything was being checked and we had Republican sources and, of course, "Deep Throat". Nixon was a brilliant man, though.'

'So was it worth all the effort of destroying him?'

'That's what some people ask, especially Europeans. They say it was only a bit of lying and all Governments lie, all Governments steal. It wasn't just that. What they were trying to do was undermine the whole democratic process . . . trying to stay in power by dirty tricks and nefarious schemes, not leaving the decision to the electors.'

'Is the *Post* going to continue its tradition of investigative journalism?'

'We have to see that the truth comes out. Lawyers aren't always too keen on the truth emerging, and a good many Government officials are lawyers. And remember the enormous number of speeches and press conferences they have to get the people to think what the Government thinks, or tell them what the Government thinks they ought to know!

'We have to be careful, though – we must only go for the big fish. When we find the Pentagon has paid $600 for a lavatory seat, for instance, we must be careful to flush out the man really responsible.'

Mrs Graham had made a rare joke. 'If we edit papers and decide not to upset anybody, I don't think it would lead either to reader loyalty or readability.

'Of course, the Government are trying to get a new information act. They want less information to be brief. They want to exempt security agents from having to divulge information, and then to exempt anything the department concerned doesn't want to tell about. But we don't have your Official Secrets Act, or your restrictive libel laws. We must still have the freest press in the world.

'The Pentagon wants to introduce lie detectors to stop leaks. Governments don't realize most leaks come from their own side, as the result of internal disagreement. It's up to them to keep their own secrets. It's not our fault if everyone leaks.'

I told Mrs Graham that the most successful new play in London was a sustained attack on the newspaper world. Did people really hate it so much?

'Of course. They view us as being arrogant. They don't like seeing microphones stuck in the faces of people at times of tragedy, or newspapermen staked out on lawns. Nor the idea of journalists being rich people with famous names. That's why I'm all for staying offstage.'

Mrs Graham gave one of her rare, charming smiles. 'And avoiding interviews like this.'

'What can we do about our unpopularity?'

'We can explain ourselves more, be readier to correct errors. Also we can be more compassionate and make sure we only choose important things to pick on.'

Since her husband's death, Katharine Graham has devoted herself to her large family. She denied the improbable rumour that she and Mr Edward Heath were smitten with each other and enjoyed candle-lit dinners. But when the story was announced, she rang her great friend, Henry Kissinger, whom she regards as 'extraordinary', and told him to 'move over'.

She is accused of enjoying opera, iced water and abstract art. She certainly enjoys her family and her homes in Long Island, Washington and Virginia. But she says that what she likes most is working. 'I care about what I'm doing.'

What she cares about most is undoubtedly her daily paper. The *Post* only circulates around Washington. 'We are very careful about that. All our advertising is geared to the area. We rely on home deliveries, not on sales in the streets. Our readers are sophisticated and print-orientated. We try and tell people what they need to know in a democracy, where the issues are so complicated they can't just rely on the simple facts given by radio and TV.'

Confined or not to the Washington area, the *Post* ranks with *The New York Times* as one of America's most influential papers. Liberal or not, it enshrines the virtues Mrs Graham also inherited from her wealthy Jewish father and Lutheran mother, fundamental beliefs she also shared with her late husband in 'education and an egalitarian society'. And she has added to this her own determination to search out and expose looneytunes wherever they may be skulking.

Chaos in the Classroom

WILLIAM GOLDING

During the 1940s, the Headmaster of Bishop Wordsworth's school in Salisbury introduced a measure of self-government into some lessons for his ten-year-old pupils. They were allowed to mount a discussion: two sides would argue, one of the boys would act as Chairman. However, an adult was to supervise such classes. One day, a Mr Golding, the English master, by way of social experiment, withdrew his supervision and gave the class complete freedom. His darkest suspicions were confirmed: he intervened just in time to prevent, as he says, mayhem and murder breaking out. Mankind, and particularly boykind, it seems, has immense powers for evil.

No doubt the boys soon got back to their seats, straightening their ties and licking their wounds, and William Golding used the experience to write *Lord of the Flies*, one of the best, and most taught, novels published since the war. His deepseated belief in original sin thus confirmed, he went on to write ten other novels and to join Rudyard Kipling, Bertrand Russell, Galsworthy and Winston Churchill – the few Englishmen to win the Nobel prize for literature. Seldom can a single period of Junior English have produced such fruitful results.

'Ring road round Salisbury,' said William Golding on the telephone, 'then Coombe Bissett, Stratford Tony, Bishopstone, Broad Chalke and Bowerchalke . . .' In the pub they told me it was the most haunted valley in Wiltshire, but the inhabitants were unimpressed by celebrities. Garbo attracted little attention when she called on Cecil Beaton at Broad Chalke, and the new Nobel laureate was known as 'Mr Scruffy' when he taught at Bishop Wordsworth's.

It was an inept description. William Golding appeared in well-pressed cotton trousers and a sweater. A mutual friend had told me to expect Mr Peggotty, the seafaring man from *David Copperfield*. What I found was more like Shaw's Captain Shotover, a sturdy 72-year-old with the white hair and beard of a minor prophet. I remembered he must be the only living English novelist to have commanded a ship in battle.

'My father was the Headmaster of Marlborough Grammar. I would say he was a great man in reduced circumstances. His views were exactly the same as those of H. G. Wells. He had great faith in evolution, Socialism and human progress. His father had been a religious Quaker cobbler, and when I put my head over the parapet at the age of eleven, I saw that atheism wasn't enough. I mean, I do remember going into a church when I was very young and telling God to strike me dead if he existed. He didn't oblige, but I did come to believe in a God as my grandfather did.'

'And your mother?'

'She was a suffragette. She stood on the steps of Marlborough Town Hall and had tomatoes thrown at her. She didn't have as much influence on me as my father. She lived a rich fantasy life.'

'How did you know that?'

'From certain things she said when she was an old woman and talked to herself.'

If William Golding was Captain Shotover, we weren't exactly in *Heartbreak House*. He lives in a rambling, whitewalled, thatched, low-ceilinged home. There was a Bechstein grand piano in the room, covered with books and scores. We sat looking out of huge picture windows as the sun came out tentatively over the Wiltshire hills and we drank white Côtes du Rhône before lunch. 'We'll follow the example of Jesus,' William Golding had said, 'and save the best wine till later.' Somewhere offstage Mrs Golding was answering the constantly ringing telephone and arranging visits from Spanish and Portuguese television units.

'You've lived in this part of the country all your life,' I said. 'Do you love it?'

'Look. I'm used to it. At times I'm frightfully bored by it. At times I'm staggered by its beauty. Often I'm toothached by its drabness. It's all to do with the weather.'

'You went on to Brasenose. Were you happy at Oxford?'

'No. I must say "no".' Golding was thoughtful.

'Why was that?'

'I wanted to write poetry, but when it came to it I had – I can't say this in Greek, but their expression is "I had an ox on my tongue". I taught myself Greek but I find I'm forgetting it. It's very alarming.'

'You tried to write poetry?'

'Oh, God, yes. Loads of it. Not much good, though. One thing I rather liked. It began like Blake, you know, "Hear the voice of the Bard!" ' and he recited:

> 'Hear the voice of the Bard!
> Ever since I left school,
> I've been three kinds of genius
> And forty kinds of fool,
> And when I get to seventy
> I'll look back and see . . .
> The geniuses weren't geniuses
> And the fools were forty-three.'

William Golding stroked his beard and laughed. 'It wasn't such a bad bit of verse, after all. Also I was a Grammar School boy. Only one undergraduate in twenty was. I suppose we felt a little uncomfortable.'

'I can't believe that . . .' I thought back to the unacceptable face of the Brideshead tradition.

'Oh yes. You can be a Socialist because you went to a Public School. For me to be a Socialist would seem to show a certain social envy.'

'But are you a Socialist?'

'I suppose that's what I'd sooner vote than anything else. But I've gradually seen that Socialism means less and less. Now I'm seventy-two, it happily doesn't much matter if I vote or not. When I was at Oxford the poets I admired were left-wing, but I found myself supremely uninterested in tractors. I must tell you, I have no political generosity.'

After Oxford, influenced by an undergraduate friend named Adam Bittlestone, William Golding lived in a Christian community in North London, studied the works of Rudolph Steiner and taught in a Rudolph Steiner school. He also became an amateur stage director and actor performing, improbably, in the works of Noël Coward and playing Danny, the central character of Emlyn Williams's *Night Must Fall*, a psychopath who keeps a head in a hat-box.

'We lived at 1001 Finchley Road,' he said refilling our glasses, 'and I thought the number must have some great mystic significance. It was a very esoteric sort of place, and I think I must have loafed about there in a sort of daze. I was also mixed up in various forms of vice, but let's draw a veil over that.'

'Please. Let's not.'

'Well. Shall we say I became obsessively interested in any girl who was prettier than the average, and I did drink a considerable number of pints of beer.'

Oh well, I thought, so much for original sin and the innate malignity of mankind.

'Didn't your father disapprove of all this Christianity?'

'Oh yes. We used to have terrific arguments about cosmology.

I mean, I said that the universe must have been created because it had a beginning. And he said I couldn't prove it had a beginning at all.'

'So what did you say?'

'That if the universe didn't start, infinite time has already passed so we couldn't have got where we are. And he said, "Just suppose time is asymptotic in a backward direction!" '

'Asym—, what was that again?'

'A line that continually approaches a curve but never reaches it. So time never got to a beginning at all.'

'What did your mother say to all that?'

'I don't think she took any part in the conversation.'

I began to see why Mrs Golding senior lived a rich inner life.

'The Navy in the war must have seemed a long way from the Theosophists in 1001 Finchley Road.'

'It was. I was a rating, and then they gave us an exam and asked us a question about explosions. My uncle had been a miner and I'd read a chapter in one of his books about dynamite, so I wrote an entire essay on the subject. I suddenly found myself acclaimed as a great expert and sent to work with all the nobs. I met Lord Cherwell and Churchill and a lot of sycophantic Brigadiers. Then an experiment went wrong and I was nearly blown up. I asked to go back to sea. I commanded a rocket carrier.'

'Did you kill anyone?'

'Oh, I suppose so. But they were a long way off. The Navy's a very gentlemanly business. You fire at the horizon to sink a ship, and then you pull people out of the water and say, "Frightfully sorry, old chap." I'd stand on the bridge like Noël Coward in *In Which We Serve* and say: "Salvoes!" and they'd answer, "Salvoes, sir!" You know, during the Normandy invasion I actually think I fired rockets on Proust's beach.'

'But you fought in a naval battle?'

'At Walcheren. On the Scheldt. Twenty-four assault craft went in and twenty-three were sunk. Do you know, it was so cold that when I smiled, the smile actually froze on my face. So all through that terrible battle I simply couldn't unfreeze my smile and the crew said: "Look at that. The old man's enjoying it!"

'Of course, I was scared stiff. But you know what I remember about the war, we laughed a lot. I told that to a young woman and she said it was hysteria and I said, not at all, we laughed at the amazing cock-ups that went on all the time. But I came out with a great respect for the Navy, and even now I can't see a naval ship without being enormously moved.'

The sea and shipwrecks, these things play a great part in William Golding's books. No doubt he not only remembers naval battles but a collision between his own boat and a Japanese cargo ship in the foggy Channel which might have been fatal. We are in danger of drowning, as we are in danger because we all live, like men at sea, too close to each other and, as he has written at the end of *Rites of Passage*, 'too close thereby to all that is monstrous under the sun and moon'.

'I wrote *Lord of the Flies* after the war,' he said. 'I remembered the class at Bishop Wordsworth's, and I remembered the gangs of Russian children after the Revolution who roamed the streets murdering people. I wanted to say to the English: "You think you've won the war and defeated Nazism so you're all nice, decent people. But look out. The evil is in us all." '

'You mean original sin?'

'You know, St Augustine was a twin. I don't really like St Augustine, but I remember that he wrote that his first memory was of trying to push his twin away from their mother's breast. I know I'm born with a great capacity for evil, and a warped ability to enjoy it.'

'Do you think we'll always be like that?'

'I don't know. We've had Neanderthal Man and *Homo sapiens*. Perhaps one day we'll get to *Homo moralis*. Perhaps we're like the ants – damned to produce a perfect society.'

'But you think there is a civilizing influence which can control our destructive urges. Where do you think that influence comes from?'

'Your guess is as good as mine.' We were having lunch then, and William Golding poured out the Chassagne-Montrachet which he had kept, on biblical advice, till later. 'I just hope I don't know.'

Mrs Golding sat at the end of the table, grey-haired, still pretty, and smiling. They had met on a committee for aid to Spain, and been married for more than forty years. She is, as she says, 'one of the left-over Left', and her husband thinks she was 'the reddest of the Reds'. She had cooked a ham large enough to feed several Spanish and Portuguese television crews in the days to come.

'Do you still want to write poetry?' I asked Golding.

'I do it a little. In Latin. You can't be fashionable in Latin.'

'Isn't it satisfying enough to write good prose?'

'Poetry's different. Poetry's on a higher level. "Now sleeps the crimson petal, now the white . . ." I still remember all the poems everyone else learnt at my Dame's School. That's what I mind about. No one's ever going to learn Golding.'

After lunch Golding sat at the piano and attacked a hugely difficult piece of Liszt until the sweet Muscat dessert wine got in the way of his fingers and he gave up, smiling. The sky was darkening over the Wiltshire hills, perhaps the landscape was about to become toothachingly dull.

'What about immortality?'

'I believe some people can have it. People who want it,' Golding said. 'It's not for me. No way!'

He moved to the sofa and refilled my glass for the last time. He was, after all, celebrating a proud moment of enormous triumph for an English writer, and I thought, not for the first time, that a deeply pessimistic view of the human condition is an excellent recipe for a happy life.

'God exists outside time,' William Golding said. 'He goes on for ever. But I don't have to. Good heavens! I'd die of boredom.'

Would You Buy a Second-hand Symphony from Him?

ANDRÉ PREVIN

Which future conductor of the Royal Philharmonic Orchestra once played 'Tiger Rag' during the Crucifixion and was consequently fired?

The answer, of course, is André Previn. It did happen a long time ago, when he was a tired teenager strumming the piano to old silent movies in a Hollywood cinema. But it could not have occurred in the early life of Solti or Karajan; it comes from a past which makes Mr Previn somehow different, and suspected of a certain levity in the solemn halls of classical music.

So he is *Private Eye*'s Mr Preview. He does commercials and appears, amid banks of endlessly repeated Grenadier Guards, to announce in a stunned sort of way that he has discovered what is probably the greatest television set in the world. He is a jazz pianist who rose to fame writing film music. Does some feeling linger in the stuffiest musical circles that you shouldn't buy a used Haydn symphony from a fellow like that?

I discovered Mr Previn on a wet Sunday morning in the woods round his house in a Surrey village. He came indoors and his wife, Heather, helped him out of an anorak which seemed not to unbutton, but to tear apart like the clothes worn by strippers and quick-change artists. He sat on the sofa, a short man whose grey hair is brushed forward in the sort of cut favoured in the swinging sixties, peering out from behind huge horn-rims with the expression of an extremely intelligent dormouse.

'My father was a very good amateur pianist,' he said, as he recalled his comfortable childhood in Berlin, where he was born in 1929, the youngest child of a well-to-do criminal lawyer. 'One of my earliest memories was of sitting under the piano while my father played through the standard German repertoire, Beethoven, Brahms, Schubert. We always had chamber music in the house. All the great symphonies are arranged in Germany for four hands and my father and I used to sit down at the piano and play them together. He insisted on my being able to sight-read. Of course we made mistakes all the time, but we got through them.'

There is a story that André was taken by his father to a double-bill consisting of *Salome* and *Coppelia* and, as a result, thought for a long time that John the Baptist had been executed in a toy shop. Soon, however, the family's safe, professional life was to end.

'We were Jewish and we had to leave Berlin when I was nine. We left at a day's notice. We abandoned a comfortable home and had no house and no money. We stayed in Paris for a little while and I went to the Conservatoire. Then we went to Los Angeles, where my father had a second cousin. We lived in terrible, coldwater apartments. Of course, my father never practised law again. He lived by giving piano lessons, which must have been very bitter for him.'

'What did your father think of your success?'

'My mother said he was proud of me and I suppose he was. But he was very Germanic and didn't like to show emotions. The first decent season I had I conducted the Philharmonic in New York and at Cleveland, Philadelphia and Minneapolis. When I told him, all he said was: "So they didn't want you at Boston, then?" '

'Success came to you fairly early?'

'It was hard at first. I knew French and German but not a word of American. The first day I arrived at school they said, "We put our lunch-packs in the back room" and I just smiled and did nothing. I was punished but I didn't know what they were talking about.

'Of course I was having lessons and playing the piano the whole time. I was the sort of weird child who enjoys practising. At five I knew I wanted to be a musician, and at fifteen I knew I wanted to be a conductor. Music's a wonderful gift, but the best gift of all is to know exactly what you want to do from your earliest childhood. To have one goal and never have any doubts about it.

'I was a professional pianist from the age of sixteen. I played at a dancing academy and I demonstrated the electric organ in a department store. I was a rehearsal pianist for ballets and musicals. Then I accompanied revivals of silent movies.

'Was it *Intolerance* which switched between biblical times and the twenties? Anyway that was the one where I stopped watching and went on playing jazz during the Crucifixion.'

'Then came the jobs for the movies?'

'It was before television got going and in the cinema anything that flickered was making money. It all needed music. I was writing for orchestras when I was sixteen, although to call those scores third-rate would be charitable. By the time I was eighteen I was conducting. Sometimes I'm watching TV when I can't sleep and those films come on at 2 a.m. and I want to hide in shame.

'I was very confident when I was a teenage conductor. I used to think I could conduct the *Missa Solemnis* because I knew the dots. Now if I have to do it, I'm frightened shitless.'

Writing film music brought Mr Previn four Oscars ('If those doorstops are important') and – I remember – marriage (his second) to Dory Previn, the sad lyricist who sang about the hell of Hollywood.

In the great wastes of Hollywood film music there were small, secret oases. 'The town was full of marvellous musicians who'd left great symphony orchestras for the sake of swimming-pools and an extremely easy life. But they were fed to the teeth with the work they were doing, and they used to meet at weekends and play classical music to themselves in abandoned school halls. Sometimes they let me conduct them.'

It was an attractive picture. These little pockets of resistance to the world of Henry Mancini, playing the 'Jupiter' Symphony underground.

'Perhaps I left it too late to leave Hollywood. You only go round once in this life and you shouldn't waste time by doing anything that bores you. I really decided to leave Hollywood when I had an argument about the music for a film with a producer who shall be nameless. I asked him to read the script, and I sat watching him do it. Do you know, I saw his lips moving! I had to get out then. You can't spend your life working for people who can't read without moving their lips.

'Then Schuyler Chapin who was head of CBS heard me conduct one of the weekend orchestras. Through him I met Ronald Wilford of Columbia Artists. I said to him, "Hound me around all the small, unknown orchestras and, if I'm no good by the end of it, you can forget the idea." So that's what he did. Some of those players were pretty bad. If you're conducting a great orchestra like the London Symphony or the New York Philharmonic they're going to sound good anyway, so conducting could be thought of as the last refuge of a musical charlatan. To make a bad orchestra sound good is a real challenge.'

'How did you manage it?'

'You have to be very clear. To inflict specific musical ideas on them.

'Later, of course, the orchestras got better. I conducted at St Louis which was top of the second class, and then Texas and the LSO. I used to commute between London and Houston, as I do now between London and Pittsburgh. But I gave up Texas. It was the people, the rich orchestra patrons you had to be polite to. I found out that one millionaire had built himself a wine cellar and then flown a firm out from New York to put artificial cobwebs on his bottles. That finally finished Texas for me.'

We had half a minute's silence while Mrs Previn brought fresh coffee and I lamented the passing of those unfortunate outsiders who move their lips when reading and turn their wine cellars into sets for Hammer movies. I remembered working with Mia Farrow, the third Mrs Previn, and her habit of sitting on the floor wrapped in a sort of Indian blanket and turning her eyes to Heaven to say, 'Mozart! Wherever you are now, I love you, Mozart,' and decided not to ask where this sort of conduct would rank on a Richter scale which had, at its top end, artificial cobwebs.

'Mia's in New York. She's been living with Woody Allen. The little Vietnamese girls we adopted, Daisy, Larksong and Soon-Yi, are with her. Next year the boys want to go out and go to school in America, which is a sadness to me.'

The present Mrs Previn also has an adopted Vietnamese daughter, so the house in Surrey is not totally bereft of beautiful oriental children.

'How do orchestras differ, over the world, I mean?'

'That's a question you either can't answer or you could write a book about it. Superficially you could say the Germans are the most obedient, and the richest. Americans call you by your Christian name at the first rehearsal. English musicians must be the hardest-worked, worst-paid collection of players in the world. In America they're on a salary, in England they get paid by the work they do. That's why they have to sandwich beer commercials and film sessions in between Schubert symphonies.'

'Is it true that musicians playing the most glorious music are all busily thinking of the next pint of beer, or whether they're going to get the last train home to Sutton and Cheam?'

'They may seem like that at times, but in fact the music must have a profound effect on them. Otherwise I can't think why they'd do it. For God's sake there must be easier ways of earning a living.'

'And audiences . . .?'

'I think London audiences are the most musically educated in the world. You know what Isaac Stern said? He said playing music in America you feel you're selling a luxury item; but in England you're providing a necessity.

187

'I'd like to play a lot more contemporary music. Of course, orchestras have an instant dislike of new music. We did a Tippett piece in Pittsburgh which was a real technical killer. At the first rehearsal you can tell they're thinking: "Why the hell should we have to learn this when we can do Beethoven Seven in our sleep?" What I do with a new piece is play it straight through at the first rehearsal; don't stop for mistakes. Then the players get to know the work as a whole, and they may even like it.

'When I'm going to do a concert, I spend about a month studying the score. I walk in the woods here but that's just to go over the lines – to make sure I know the words, you could say. I don't conduct entirely from memory. I like to have the score there but I don't often turn the pages. When it's something I've done a lot of times before I try to think if there's a new way of doing it.

'I don't know whether you know about a conductor's life? Well, actors are always wondering if they'll be back on the end of the pier or drawing the dole after the current engagement. My diary's full for the next four years. I know that on a Thursday in October 1984 I'll be rehearsing the Mahler Five in Vienna at 10 a.m. Recently I got a call from the Concertgebouw and I asked Heather if she'd like to go to Amsterdam, and she said, "I'd love to. When?" and I told her, "In the Spring of 1985." '

Orchestra players like André Previn. They find him articulate and friendly; he understands their problems and they have a great respect for him as a pianist and a practical musician. When the quarrelsome but magnificent LSO was down on its luck he brought them a lot of new recording sessions, and they still remember their early Rachmaninov recordings with him with particular pride.

Strangely, in spite of his early life with Beethoven and love of Mozart, it's conducting the later Romantic composers that seems to be his strength. Only a few players have doubts as to whether he can express his considerable musicianship as well through his body, as a conductor, as he can through a piano. No one doubts his sincerity or the dedication which led him to abandon the lush pastures of Los Angeles.

Mr Previn came up with a thought which seemed scarcely original, but then he said: 'I tell you what. Every work of art is always greater than any possible performance of it. You play it as well as you can but it's still there, better than you can make it. Well, that suggests some sort of mystery. At least it enforces humility.'

It was time to go. The children wanted their lunch, the piano was awaiting, and there was a pale sunshine in the Surrey woods where Mr Previn would walk to remember the lines.

Cuisine Determinée

ANTON MOSIMANN

'I was an only child. My parents had a restaurant. It was 150 seats at Nidau in Switzerland. Good bourgeois cooking. I think the customers probably ate too much, plenty of *rösti*. I lived in the restaurant, did my homework at one of the tables, everything. It was an unusual childhood. I was very happy. I started cooking at the age of six, cheese fondue and spaghetti bolognese. I loved to do that. Later, when my parents closed the restaurant and took a day off I used to cook for friends, not just other children but grown-ups. When I was twelve I fell in love with a car, and I said to myself, "Anton," I said, "how can you earn enough money to buy that car?" Listen, this will show you that I have achieved success because of my drive and determination in life. I collected worn-out bulbs and sold their metal holders. I sold old newspapers. I bought live rabbits in the market, brought them home and hit them behind the ears with a steel bar, and then I sold them to the butchers. By the time I was eighteen I was able to buy my car! It was a white Triumph sports. A two-seater. It cost me 8,750 francs.

'I came of three generations of chefs. When I was fifteen I had to leave home to become an apprentice at the Hotel Baeren at Twann. We worked fourteen to fifteen hours a day. I did every-thing, scrubbed the floor, cleaned the copper dishes. I had one day off a week and I spent that at college learning to cook. I used to sit up in my room at night and cry. I said to myself, "Anton, you deserve better than this. This job's not big enough for you." So I went to the Palace Hotel, Villars. I was a *commis*, running between one station and the other. We weren't meant to go out but I used to leave my best suit in the garage and say, "I'm just stepping out for a breath of air," and quickly change out of my chef's jacket. There was a girl in another hotel. I knew she existed and I found her. I used to help in the kitchen garden and the vineyard, anything to do with cooking. I always loved it. You like this rosette?' Mr Mosimann looked down at the parcel of smoked salmon containing an avocado mousse and topped with a dollop of caviare and took a modest sip of champagne. 'This the Queen had at the banquet last night.'

Anton Mosimann, still only thirty-eight, has been *Maître Chef des Cuisines* at the Dorchester Hotel for the last nine years. He cooks what he proudly calls '*Cuisine Naturelle*'; but his extraordinary self-confidence and single-minded devotion to his career might have made it '*Cuisine Determinée*'. He is a trim and athletic man who dreams of new recipes, mousse of brill with sea-urchin sauce, *médaillons de foie gras au vin rouge*, as he jogs round Holland Park before breakfast. He is prematurely bald with a greying fringe of hair and a moustache. His eyes are small and very bright, quick to spot a button off the jacket on one of his eighty-five chefs, a foot of unwashed floor or a curdling sauce. He talks in rapid, almost too correct English with the sharp flavour of a German-Swiss accent. It's easy to imagine the brisk tones in which, all his life, he has been saying, 'Anton, you deserve better than this,' and sending himself off on another punishing Swiss cookery course or to a job as a humble *commis pâtissier* at Gstaad because he decided his pastry was imperfect. Now, with five diplomas (including 'Dietary Studies' and 'Carving and Flambé'), a number of Gold Medals and at the top of his profession, he can presumably give Anton a few words of quiet congratulation. He is, after all, the only chef to have had his birthday listed in *The Times*.

'When I was eighteen a friend asked me to join him at the Cavalieri Hilton in Rome. I was afraid I was too young, but I went, in my car! It was a wonderful time for me. I was a *commis* in charge of the larder. Then I had control of the cold section, of the salads and the buffet. We used to leave work at eleven o'clock at night and go and have a drink. Then we would drive to the seaside and swim at four o'clock in the morning. I tell you. I was young and strong. I did wrestling. I had a beautiful car. Girls came to me automatically.'

'Do girls like chefs?' I had a vision of bevies of eager receptionists pursuing gentlemen in tall, white hats.

'I think so. Yes. If you are a chef your aim is to give pleasure. Happy faces make me happy. I believe girls respond to that. Anyway, I must say, I had a rather colourful life. They were all nice girls. All over the world.'

'Do you like Italian food?'

'I love it!'

'The best cooking comes from peasant traditions, where the ingredients are very simple?'

'Italian. Chinese. Yes. Natural ingredients. I love the French bourgeois food at the Brasserie Lipp in Paris.'

'And English?'

'English, yes. Boiled beef and carrots! You have the best markets here. The best materials. Billingsgate. I think it is as good as the fish market in Tokyo! You can see everything you buy. Now this is a chicken consommé made with fresh coriander and parsley. It comes with a pastry covering so it will keep very hot for you!' And we settled down to the simple things in life, with the help of a bottle of Vieux-Château-Certan, Pomerol, 1970.

He had been kind enough to invite me to lunch in his private dining-room, a tiny enclosure by the huge, booming kitchens in the catacombs beneath the Dorchester. Around us numbers were being called, plates and entrée dishes were clattering, and Anton Mosimann in an impeccable white jacket, a carefully sharpened pencil in his tall hat, had been striding up and down like a captain on the bridge, supervising the midday meal for the retinue of the Emir of Qatar, who, the night before, had entertained the Queen. The operation had gone smoothly, the lunchtime storm was over, and the distant shouts for shashlik and grilled chicken had died away. So, now the *Maître des Cuisines* was relaxing and being waited on by an attentive steward in a white jacket with gold epaulettes. We reached the main course, a small fillet steak poached in beef bouillon on a nest of crisp, barely cooked, ginger flavoured vegetables with a *coulis* of tomatoes flavoured with horseradish. I thought how impossible it is to write about food without sounding like an American menu, and of the Ethiopian masses squatting down, if they are very lucky, to a handful of morning-dropped corn from Oxfam.

'Hunger in the world? Of course I want to help. I tell you. I came out of the Dorchester one night; it was pouring with rain and there was an open car. I spent a long time covering that car up, although I didn't know who it belonged to. My instinct is to help people, you see.'

'Don't you feel you're always working for the rich? How much does lunch cost at the Dorchester?'

'It needn't be so much. You can do it for £15 a head. They are not all rich. Sometimes it's people who save up for treats.'

'What does a great chef need?'

'You need instinct. You must have the feeling of just when that piece of meat is done. You must have a flair for colour, like a painter, so you can choose the patterns food makes on the plate. It's no good having just that or you would put strawberries with sole, which would be awful, so you must remember all your tastes. And you must be calm, dead calm!'

'I thought great chefs were fat and temperamental and chased the *commis* with knives.'

'No more. I cooked with one like that at St Moritz. He was eighty-seven and had worked with the great Escoffier. He used to fall asleep over the stoves and drink a lot of champagne and was always stealing people's knives and selling them. He did once attack a customer who came to complain . . . But that's all over! My chefs have mineral water to drink, which is very nice for them. I tell you, seventy-five per cent of them are British and they are very good. Every morning, at the start of the day, I shake hands with everyone. I say, "Hullo, Henry," "Hullo, George," whatever their names are. I have my wonderful gift of motivating people. I am the father to all of them!'

'Do you compose your recipes in the kitchen, or are you thinking all the time?'

'Oh, all the time! I have four thousand cookery books, but I think of recipes when I am in the car – now I have an antique 1936 Vauxhall – and when I am jogging. I remember the exact taste of scallops and I think of something new to do with them, not drown them in Noilly Prat, that's for certain.'

'And you see the colour on plates?' Octagonal plates, decorated with open mussels and shrimps, artfully placed lettuce leaves and swirls of sauce, photographed from above provide the artwork in Mr Mosimann's books and on the walls of his dining-room.

'Constantly. I create colours. I mix sweet and sour. I feel my way through, trying for something new and then relax. It suddenly comes. Beautiful! It's very creative.'

'Of course, it's a short-lived creation?' Not many poems, pictures or sonatas get consumed by the end of the lunch and finally disposed of in some of the best bathroom suites in Europe.

'That's right. Poof! It's gone. Nothing left. That's why the only thing to do is to love the people that eat it.'

'After Rome I had to choose whether to go for money, that is work in a canteen or for an airline, or to get to the top of my profession. I always wanted to do better so I went back to school in Switzerland. Then I went to the Queen Elizabeth hotel in Montreal where I had flat with a swimming-pool and a sauna. I was executive *sous* chef, I was number two, but I wanted to be head chef so I went back to school again. Later I went to the Palace Hotel, St Moritz, where we cooked on coal. You had to change your white jacket three or four times a day.

'I applied for a job at the Swiss Pavilion at Expo '70 in Japan. I found the Government knew all about me and they asked me to be a head chef.'

Two important things happened to Anton Mosimann in Japan. He became interested in the naturalness and lightness of Japanese food and on the plane he met a girl called Kathrin, the Swiss Pavilion's housekeeper, who became his wife. Now they have two sons, a flat in Ennismore Gardens and a cottage in the country. He is up early, jogging or going to the markets; he arrives at work at 8.30 in the morning and doesn't leave until after 10 o'clock at night. During the day he has a formal meeting with his *chefs de partie*, fixes the menus with his clerk and cooks for three or four hours, helping out, demonstrating, tasting incessantly from a small teaspoon.

'I had sleepless nights, wondering if I could really do without butter and cream in my *Cuisine Naturelle*! Now we poach a lot, or steam or grill. We never fry except in non-stick pans without any fat, of course. Are we right? Who can tell what is right in cooking? You may like a lot of salt, I may like less salt. It is all a matter of taste. All I know is that it is a crime to overcook, and there is never an excuse for a bad meal.'

The influence of *Cuisine Minceur* seemed to me to come upon the world like a blight, being an excuse for small portions, food that had lost the taste of its natural origins and the appalling kiwi fruit creeping into everything like a plague of termites. It became impossible, except in a few determined outposts, to buy a sole that wasn't plaited, or curled and doused in a pink liquid. Roast duck meant two minute slivers accompanied by a few black grapes and a leaf of raw cabbage. The usual rewards of gluttony, added weight and a pleasing feeling of surfeit, were no longer to be had for the astronomical price of a restaurant bill. Not only did the great English dishes vanish, not only was steak and kidney pudding anathema in this country, but solid French bourgeois cooking became hard to find in France.

Anton Mosimann's natural cuisine is a distinct improvement on the recent past. The food tastes of its ingredients, which he touches and feels on his dawn visits to Billingsgate and Smithfield. He buys what is the best available and adjusts his menus properly to the seasons. Furthermore the splendours of English cooking have not been forgotten. We ended lunch with bread and butter pudding, Mr Mosimann's speciality, handed down from the safe world of the old English nursery.

What use can be made of Anton Mosimann's discoveries in the ordinary household, thawing a pizza under the microwave in order to watch *Dynasty*? He has gone on the road, watched by television, to advise a Sheffield couple on how to cook their bread and butter pudding on a tray with a newspaper soaked in water to make it taste like a soufflé. He has worked out how an excellent dinner for four – beef and lentil soup and braised rabbit – need cost no more than £3·11p. All the same, many of his recipes involve a great many little items such as fresh-water crayfish, morels, raw foie gras, sea urchins and caviare. Splendid as all these ingredients are, they're not to be found in the friendly neighbourhood Tescos.

Cooking at the Mosimann level must remain a rare treat, and dinner at the Dorchester – which is most likely to come in at around £37 a head – must be a celebration and a bit of an orgy. In these circumstances I wonder if we really need to be told that it's so healthy and good for us. Does the occasional blow-out need to be therapeutic, like jogging?

However this may be, there is no denying Anton Mosimann's extraordinary self-confidence, not to be found in any playwright, novelist or painter known to me, and his devotion to his art. As we walked out of his underground fiefdom, past huge bottles of peaches and home-made vinegar, I asked if he had any regrets about his chosen profession. 'Regrets? Never. Every day is wonderful. I tell you, I feel proud every time I put on my chef's jacket.'

The Romantic Lawyer

LORD SCARMAN

'I'm a romantic optimist about the law. I believe it can always be reformed to make it better.'

Leslie Scarman sat in his room in the House of Lords and gazed thoughtfully out of the window at his favourite view of Westminster Abbey. The books and papers were being stacked on chairs, the pictures had been taken down ('I always tried to make it look as little like a lawyer's room as possible,' Lord Scarman said) and the removal men were expected. The large Victorian Gothic clock ticked on remorselessly. At the age of seventy-four, after eight years as a Law Lord, twenty-nine years as a Judge and half a century as a barrister, Lord Scarman was retiring. He looked forward to nothing particular to do except live near Canterbury, read the *Odes* of Horace, listen to Verdi operas, get to know his grandchildren better, sit in the House of Lords ('As a liberal radical with a small "l" and a small "r",' he says) and reform the British Constitution.

His departure will rob the Law Courts of one of their most sympathetic and enlightened Judges. But it's strange that a man who scored a double First in Classics at Oxford, who was the Harmondsworth Law Scholar of his year, who must be one of the few lawyers who can read Pericles' speech to the Athenians in Greek and is not only a Privy Councillor but a recipient of the Russian Battle Order of Merit, is probably best known to the public because on 10 April 1981 a number of discontented and frustrated black youths started a riot in Atlantic Road, Brixton.

'I will tell you a little about my life, but not too much. I was born in Streatham, strangely enough only a few miles from Brixton.' Lord Scarman smiled as though the riot area had become, in some strange way, also his home. 'My father was an insurance broker at Lloyd's.'

'So the family weren't poor?'

'Comfortably off. My grandfather was a complete Cockney who worked at Waring & Gillow, the London department store, but he had a French wife, a Protestant from the Jura. My father was a very kind man, but my mother was the stronger character. She was very ambitious for her children. They were both very middle class and determined – and this included my sister – that we should be properly educated.'

'You went to Radley. Did you enjoy that?'

'I can't say my schooldays were the happiest days of my life but I enjoyed it for two reasons. One I started my humanitarian education in the Classics. Two I had my music.'

'Did you play an instrument?'

'The B flat tenor trombone.' The answer was immediate but unexpected.

'It seems an odd choice.'

'As a choirboy my treble voice had been very good. When it broke, it became clear to me that it was not so good, so I wanted to play something. Sydney Watson, my old Head of Music, consulted the bandmaster. "It's no good Leslie taking up the piano," he said, "he's always working at his books and won't keep it up. He won't have enough time to practise the violin so it had better be brass." Up spake the bandmaster, "I need a B flat tenor trombone." So I played it in an orchestra for six years and enjoyed it greatly. And nowadays I'm an opera fanatic.'

'When did that start?'

'I can tell you specifically. Date, 1944. Place, liberated Rome.

Occasion, a concert given to the Allied Commanders by the hereditary Mayor of Rome. The work, *Butterfly*. It was exactly right for
my romantic temperament. Now I love Verdi and Mozart operas.
I find Wagner too overwhelming.'

'And when did it first occur to you that you might be a barrister?'

'When I was fifteen and I read the life of Marshall Hall. As I
say, my feelings about it were entirely romantic; I had no interest
in the law at all. I wanted to be a great advocate.'

Marjoriebanks's magnificent life of the Great Advocate, who
conducted the defence in some of the choicest Victorian and
Edwardian murder cases rather in the manner that Sir Henry Irv-
ing was playing Hamlet at the Lyceum, must be the book that has
won more recruits than any other to the legal profession. Many
become disappointed when they discover that it's inappropriate to
do Sir Edward Marshall Hall's moving speech about the Scales of
Justice during a routine company winding-up in the Chancery
Division.

'No. Classics and Ancient History. I still read a great deal of the
prose, Cicero and Tacitus. I enjoy Aristophanes very much, but
Horace is my bedside reading.'

Scarman started to practise at the bar in 1936, when he was
twenty-five and living on his scholarship.

'I was a pupil of Basil Blagden who ended as a humble County
Court Judge. Blagden was a great eccentric who would carry a joke
beyond all reason. For instance he included on his income tax
return "the sum of one shilling and sixpence gained by pressing
button 'B' in a telephone kiosk". I used to crew his yacht and we
once collided with a Dutch tramp steamer while Blagden stood on
the deck lecturing the captain on the legal right of way. Although
he was undoubtedly correct in law we were made of wood and the
Dutchman was made of iron so we eventually hobbled back to port
and sank.

'Then the war came and I was an administrative officer in

Bomber Command in North Africa. It was very searing, so many people killed. Then Tedder came out and they wanted to give him a Court Martial warrant; they said a Commander had to have the power of life and death over his men. He said he was far too busy fighting the war to bother about Courts Martial so he found this strange lawyer Scarman and he said, "I don't want your opinion. All you are required to do is correspond with the Air Ministry until they drop the idea." I did and they dropped it. Tedder took me with him to Berlin when we accepted the German surrender.

'I came out of the RAF and started making a living at the bar. I was very thorough in my work; I was the only barrister who did an inquest and insisted on meeting the corpse. I admired Patrick Hastings as a wonderful cross-examiner – that was about all he did as he left most of his cases to his juniors – and I admired Norman Birkett for his mellifluous voice and way of handling the jury in cases like the Brighton Trunk murders. But I realized I could never be a great theatrical advocate like them, so, for the first time, I turned my attention to the law.'

'Would you say that your romantic feelings aren't attached to the individual case but to the idea of law itself?'

'You've got me absolutely right. The law is a great power in our lives; it can be a power for good or evil.'

'So if you live under evil laws, for instance in Hitler's Germany or in South Africa, it must be right to put your conscience above the law?'

'Ever since I've thought about these matters philosophically, I've had to accept that. The question is *when* it becomes right . . .'

'Do you believe in the law of nature, some absolute standard of justice?'

'If you use the language of my education I'd agree. If you said the *jus gentium*, the standards which all civilized nations have in common . . .'

'Does God come into your concept of the law at all?'

Leslie Scarman has a long intelligent face and the bright, amused eyes and full lips he may have inherited from his French ancestors. He lay back in his chair, his hands clasped, and looked at Westminster Abbey with the gentle courtesy with which he used to inspect a witness.

'I can't say I'm a religious man, to be quite honest with you.'

'You don't believe in the Great Court of Appeal beyond the sky?'

'No. Although I'm bound to say that I think it likely that God does exist, judging the matter according to the civil law on the balance of probabilities.'

'But on the strict standard of proof beyond reasonable doubt in a criminal case, God wouldn't quite get a verdict?'

'Why were you chosen for the Brixton riot inquiry?'

'I'd done the disturbances in Northern Ireland, and in Red Lion Square and at Grunwick. The findings in the Red Lion Square inquiry about keeping opposing factions a considerable distance apart had become part of police training.'

'Since Brixton we've had Hanworth. Are there any parts of your Brixton recommendations that haven't been put into practice?'

'What pleases me is that none of our Brixton recommendations was found to be false.'

'What about the new idea of a law of "disorderly conduct"?'

'I doubt whether it's necessary and the old law is perfectly sufficient.'

'You recommended that racially prejudiced or discriminating behaviour should be an offence under the Police Discipline Code . . .'

'So it is now. I introduced that clause into the Police Bill in the House of Lords and the Government adopted it in the Commons. I think the Brixton report was a catalyst.'

'But the problems are as far from solution as ever?'

'Police training has changed, and I think that's a result of Brixton. But the real causes are housing, jobs and education. Education above all.'

'Is it an answer to have more black police? Black police seem to beat up blacks just as cheerfully in South Africa as white policemen do.'

'In South Africa the blacks still think that any black who joins the police has gone over to the enemy, and they're right. Some of them may think that in Brixton, but they're not right.'

'Do you think we should have a quota of black police?'

'I'm against "quota" police officers. But I think we should give ethnic minorities all the help we can in the way of grants for education and so on to join.'

'Looking at the riots, do you think our society's actually cracking up?'

'With all our difficulties I still think this is the most tolerant and civilized country to live in in the world.'

'Why is Tom Denning so against your proposal to introduce a new Bill of Rights?'

'I don't think Tom quite understands the position. We wouldn't be taking power away from Parliament, all we're seeking to do is to make the European Convention on Human Rights part of our law.'

'Whenever I mentioned the Convention on Human Rights down at the Old Bailey the Judges used to give me a look of bored incredulity.'

'Well, it's not quite like that in the higher courts. But perhaps we all need educating . . .'

'In basic principles of liberty?'

'There's an enormous amount of administrative law now, cases in which the courts have to judge the actions of Government departments. Where can they find the principles to act? Only by searching back in eighteenth-century cases which may not be very helpful. A Bill of Rights would give them a clear set of standards . . .'

'The right to free speech, to privacy and to have a family life.

Protection from harsh and degrading punishment. Do you think being locked three in a cell with no proper sanitation amounts to harsh and degrading punishment?'

'If all I read about prisons is true I think it may be. In America there have been successful applications to the courts on that basis. But I don't think English Judges would set about making rules for schools and prisons as American Judges have.'

'Wouldn't it be a field day for lawyers? And the House of Lords would spend all its time interpreting just what the Constitution meant?'

'Eighty per cent of work in the Judicial Committee of the House of Lords is interpretive as it is.'

'What do you think is the single, greatest advantage of that sort of Constitution?'

'I think that at long, long last we might be able to erect on it a decent law of privacy.'

Lord Scarman, a very private man, spoke with considerable feeling.

'Looking back on your life, did you ever expect to be a Judge?'

'I had no judicial ambitions and it came as a total surprise. I had a big practice in planning cases, and then a large general practice. I had become very good, though I say it as shouldn't, at cross-examining expert witnesses. Then the Lord Chancellor asked me to become a Judge in the Probate, Divorce and Admiralty Division. I told him that my only qualification must have been that I was about the only barrister ever to have lost an undefended divorce case in Brighton. He said that didn't matter a bit.'

'Can a Judge look at a witness and tell immediately if he or she's telling the truth?'

'Only sometimes. I've known many witnesses who gave their evidence perfectly convincingly, and dealt quite easily with the best cross-examinations the best barristers could throw at them, and they were still lying.'

'Does the truth become clear to a Judge early on in a case?'

'How do you get at the truth? That concerned me, because I'd known so many Judges get it wrong when I was at the bar. You remember the case we were both in, *re* Fuld deceased?'

It was a will case which lawyers will never forget, mainly because it lasted about nine months and concerned the complex love and business life of a young German millionaire who died of a brain tumour. As a junior barrister I had sat looking up at the patient Mr Justice Scarman, marvelling at his grasp of detail and occasionally, it must be admitted, during the *longueurs*, thinking up sketches for *Not So Much a Programme* . . .

'I had decided by that time that what a Judge had to do was to keep quiet. So I just lay on the beach and let the waves of evidence wash over me. And then, when the tide went down, the truth became quite clear.'

'And what do you think's been your greatest achievement in the law?'

'Undoubtedly when I was Chairman of the Law Commission, advising on reform. I was determined to get rid of the defended divorce case. I'd been sickened by the spectacle of ordinary men and women having to parade the secrets of their married lives in public. I remember trying a case where a girl was terrified to admit that she'd committed adultery because she thought I'd take away her child. I kept on trying to tell her that wouldn't happen, but she didn't believe me. In the end I found her guilty of adultery and gave her custody. It was all a long, painful fight which made no difference at all to the outcome.'

The Gothic fantasy clock on the wall had ticked away my time. Lord Scarman uncurled himself from his chair and stood up, surprisingly tall and square shouldered, to see me to the lift. We walked together down the muffled corridors of a House of Lords on holiday.

'Were Judges very alarming to you when you started at the bar?'

'Quite terrifying. And I didn't know what to do about it. I didn't understand how the legal system worked.'

'And do you think the law's improved during your time in it?' I wondered if he would give any comfort to the cry for a return to so-called Victorian values. 'Have we become more reasonable, tolerant, humane?'

'Immeasurably so.' The romantic optimism was undimmed. Leslie Scarman is a Judge we can ill afford to lose, particularly if his room gets refurnished by someone who actually *wants* to make it look as though a lawyer lived there.

The Illusionist without Illusions

NORMAN TEBBIT

A visit to Norman Tebbit arouses excited expectations. Should you take a long spoon, a bulb of garlic, or two twigs roughly bound into a cross? He has been variously described as a 'semi-house-trained polecat' (Michael Foot), the 'Chingford skinhead' (a Labour MP) and, since he acquired a cottage in Devon, the 'Hound of the Baskervilles'. Would he arise creakingly from a coffin in the basement of Smith Square in a crumpled suit of tails and a scarlet-lined opera cloak? Eager for the green limelight and the sound hissing from the wings I hurried down the backstreets of Westminster.

There was no smell of sulphur in the Conservative Central Office, only the flags of the United Kingdom, a bust of Winston Churchill wearing his siren suit, large helpful girls hurrying back from lunch and a gentle, grey-haired man talking about his retirement. 'We have this big labrador dog and I think I'll devote my time to him.' And then, after a longish wait, I was ushered into the presence of the man whom the *Financial Times* could best describe as an enigma. If this were true I had only forty-five minutes of the Chairman's time to find any sort of solution.

'My father was in the retail trade when I was born in the thirties.' Mr Tebbit touched lightly on the story of his life. 'Which had the most influence on me, my mother or my father? Heavens only knows. I don't think either of them had! I think I had more influence on them. Were they Conservative? I don't think I ever asked. They weren't particularly religious. I don't think God ever came into my upbringing at all.'

'You've been very close to death at least twice.'

'My wife reckons I come close to death every time I drive a car, but I've got no convictions yet. Do go on.'

'Once when you were strapped into the cockpit of a burning Mosquito during your National Service and you had to break open the canopy to escape. Another, of course, at the time of the Brighton hotel bombing. Did you feel you came close to God on either of those occasions?'

'I would have to say, quite honestly, that I haven't met Him yet.'

'Did you learn anything about death itself?'

'I can't tell you that I saw it as a gateway to pleasure.'

'You wouldn't describe yourself as a religious man?'

'Well, I'm not an atheist. But Christ being the Son of God and so on . . .? No. I can't believe that. But I do think there's a system of order in the universe.'

'So God's a paid-up member of the Conservative Party?'

'Oh, yes. Of course.' And the suppressed laughter which had been bubbling away behind Mr Tebbit's surprising answers was released like a jet of steam. 'I've never had the slightest doubt about that. After all, he couldn't be a Socialist.'

'Why not?'

'Because of the process of evolution.'

'Tell me.'

'Well, as I've playfully pointed out, evolution meant getting rid of the dinosaurs and replacing them with some more efficient and up-to-date animals. Any Socialist would have been dedicated to protecting the dinosaurs in the name of compassion or conservation or something. The dinosaurs would never have been allowed to go. So God can't be a Socialist.'

'You mean to say that there aren't any dinosaurs in the Tory Party?'

'Of course there are.' Mr Tebbit was laughing openly now, almost blowing the lid off the kettle. 'And they've got to be got rid of too!'

We sat at a small, empty board-room table in the Chairman's office. Mr Tebbit is smaller than I had been led to believe. His face is lined, his hair thin, he blinks a good deal and he has the pallor of actors or prisoners, persons who live by artificial light. He has the look of a sardonic conjuror, an illusionist without illusions. His eyes are very bright and he sits relaxed, with his hands folded. He has clearly emerged from his own ordeal, and the deep tragedy of his wife's injuries, with his sense of humour intact. What is curious is that he seems to find his own lethal brand of politics hugely entertaining. For a moment, and unexpectedly, I remembered my father who once told me that there was a great deal of harmless fun to be got out of the Divorce Court.

'This father of *yours*. When did he actually get on his bike?'

'In the thirties. He'd lost his job as a shop manager and he went off round the building sites.'

'Round Edmonton?'

'He was looking for casual labour.'

I remembered that Mr Tebbit had made his famous remark as a riposte to Michael Heseltine (when they were shaping up as rival heirs apparent), who had suggested that more money should be spent on jobs in Liverpool. 'My father didn't riot but got on his bike to look for work.' It was perhaps more a bit of Cabinet in-fighting than serious advice to the hopelessly unemployed of Northern England. In any event Mr Tebbit's father doesn't seem to have had a great effect on his son and at this point he departed from the interview, cycling hopefully.

'When did you become a Conservative?'

'At Edmonton Grammar School. When I first read Fred . . . Oh, what's his name again?'

'Hayek.' A grey-haired, red-faced, rather tweedy amanuensis

had appeared silently and, sitting behind Mr Tebbit, supplied the name of the Austrian monetarist who seems to have exercised such a lasting influence on the boy from Edmonton. Even during his recent illness Mr Tebbit kept going by reading the work of the 'Two Freds, Hayek and Truman'. 'I read *The Road to Serfdom*. I read history from 1830 to 1914. I knew that the centrally controlled state leads to unpleasant consequences. Socialism is bound to become authoritarian.'

'But you grew up in the years of the Attlee Government. Wouldn't you agree that was a time of enormous political achievement?'

'Don't get me wrong. I'm in favour of the Health Service and equal educational opportunities.'

'And Attlee and Stafford Cripps were extremely well-intentioned and well-meaning people?'

'Well-meaning people are the most dangerous. You can't have Socialism unless you control incomes and prices. So you go the way of Hitler and Mussolini.'

'But we lived through the Labour Governments of Attlee and Harold Wilson and I never noticed many gauleiters around. I mean, not too many people got carted off by the Gestapo at dawn.'

'That's because those Socialist Governments failed. You don't know what would have happened if they'd been a success!' Mr Tebbit fell into a happy silence, relishing the thought of the Fascist state England only seems to have avoided thanks to the clumsiness of Harold Wilson.

'So after school and Hayek you wanted to go into politics?'

'Like any other ambitious young man, I wanted to succeed.' Success came to Norman Tebbit after jobs in publishing and journalism, National Service, a long stint as an airline pilot (where he was an officer of BALPA, the pilots' union) and entry to the House as Member for Epping in 1970. On the back benches he emerged as the new style of abrasive, lower-middle-class, hardline and sharp-tongued MP who would herald the greatest and perhaps most vote-catching change in Conservative history. If Norman Tebbit hadn't existed, one perceptive old Tory was heard to say, it would have been necessary to invent him.

'When you got into the House of Commons didn't you feel isolated among a lot of upper-class, old-public-school Tories?'

'To be quite honest with you, I don't think I noticed them. I did think a few of them were intellectually arrogant.' Norman Tebbit made an early impression by the savagery of his questions from the back benches. No doubt he was off on that strange quest for political power which has a fascination that has nothing to do with the free market economy.

'You talk a lot about monetarism, but money really isn't the most important thing in life, is it? I mean, you could presumably make a fortune in the City but you go on with this extremely thankless political task. It can't be for the money.'

For the first time in our conversation Mr Tebbit was silent, nor did he laugh.

'When Mrs Thatcher allowed the American planes to set off from our shores to bomb Libyans, did you expect such a hostile public reaction?'

'We thought that there might be some political repercussions. Yes.'

'Some newspapers, I think the *Daily Telegraph*, suggested that you weren't in favour of our giving permission for that. Were they right?'

'I'm in favour of everything which our Government has concluded it's in favour of.' Mr Tebbit chose his words with great care. They didn't seem to imply enormous enthusiasm for the Libyan adventure. 'The United States administration had supported us in the Falklands. It's best to be friendly with your allies.'

'I think some people find it hard to understand an American Government which says it intends to fight terrorism over here but finances and supports some particularly brutal terrorism by the Contras in Nicaragua.'

'The Contra situation is a difficult area. Certainly the Nicaraguan Government is not very democratic. I'm not prepared to say whether or not I think the United States is going about it in the right way.'

'Do you think that the British people resent our country being used as an American aircraft carrier?'

'Remember the captain of the ship is British and she had to give her permission.'

'You've said that anti-American talk is a sign of "cheap and dirty parties seeking cheap and dirty votes". But what's wrong with saying that we should be an independent force for moderation and common sense in the world and not become implicated in America's more thoughtless adventures? Is my vote dirty if that's what I think?'

'That's a perfectly reasonable position to take. I meant people who talk about Americans as they might about blacks who'd come to settle in the neighbourhood. The sort of people who chalked "Yanks Go Home" on walls during the war.'

'And perhaps we resent British businesses being sold off to America?'

'The United States don't mind us taking over their businesses, which we do quite a lot. And we never sold Westland to the Americans. It wasn't ours to sell, in spite of all they said on that terrible box in the corner.' Mr Tebbit nodded with deep disapproval at the expressionless, grey face of an unlit television set.

'Going on from what you said about "dirty votes". Is there really any future for you in abusing the other parties? I mean, to win the election you've got to capture the middle ground. Is there any sense in just saying things that'll only please the Party faithful? Presumably they'll vote for you anyway.'

'The faithful won't vote for you unless you're faithful to them. I've got to stand up for what I believe is right.'

'Didn't you emerge from the terrible ruins of that bombed hotel feeling that all the bickering and insults between political parties are rather trivial?'

'Oh no.' Mr Tebbit's eyes were twinkling and all his good spirits were restored. 'I think you come back from such experiences greatly refreshed and determined to carry on with the job in hand. And you may as well do all you can *while* you can. I feel I'm living on borrowed time anyway. I'm playing with the casino's money.'

'Why did you do so disastrously in the recent elections? And now you've sunk to third place in the polls . . .'

'I think people are pleased with what we've done. We've brought down inflation. We've seen off Galtieri and Scargill. Now they want us to do something else.'

'They want you to do something about unemployment.'

'Perhaps there's nothing that Governments *can* do about unemployment. But the 80 per cent who're in work are benefiting from higher real incomes and pensioners are benefiting from lower inflation.'

'You can't expect a man suddenly thrown out of work in Middlesborough to be much cheered up by the low rate of inflation.'

'Well, that's it. Our aims and objectives aren't being made clear to the public. Lower inflation should produce more jobs eventually, but they don't understand that.'

'Don't you think that people are quite willing to pay higher rates and taxes if it means proper education, less unemployment and better public services?'

'I believe they want all those things without having to pay for them. They want their cake and they want to eat it.'

'But if they decide they'll pay for a better sort of cake . . .'

'I don't think they've decided that. I think they agree with us about taxes but they're not clear what we mean to do next. And then there's the question of the Prime Minister herself . . .'

Mrs Thatcher, in full colour, smiled down on us from a large gilt photograph frame on the wall. Surely Mr Tebbit wasn't going to suggest that she might be an election liability?

'It's a question of her leadership when our aims aren't clearly defined. When people understand what she's doing there's a good deal of admiration for her energy and resolution and persistence, even from those people who don't agree with her. Now there's a perception that we don't know where we're going so those same qualities don't seem so attractive.'

'Isn't there also the boredom factor?'

'What?'

'Eventually we get bored with our politicians. We feel they've gone on too long. We got bored with Macmillan and Harold Wilson who were enormously admired in their time.'

'I'm not sure that people get bored. Journalists get bored. That's the trouble.'

Is that true? Or does the great British talent for boredom save us, even more than the free market economy, from the perils of dictatorship? I had another ten minutes before the Conservative Party Chairman had to rush away and see to the Duchy of Lancaster, and the enigma was still unsolved. Does he, for instance, believe his more extravagant opinions (that Labour Party Government leads to dictatorship or that other political parties are 'dirty and cheap'), or has he, by his own choice of pungent words, come to convince himself? Both may be true; he has convinced himself therefore he truly believes. There's no reason to doubt his sincerity.

'You gave a Disraeli Lecture denouncing the Permissive Society. But surely there were some worthwhile reforms during the Roy Jenkins era. You wouldn't be in favour of us still imprisoning consenting homosexuals of full age, for instance?'

'I wouldn't imprison homosexuals *as such*, no.' What on earth did the 'as such' mean? For the first time Mr Tebbit sounded gloomy. Then he cheered up and went on. 'Don't get me wrong.

I'm not intolerant or prudish. I'm nothing like Mizz Short of the Labour Party who wants to ban Page Three of the *Sun*. I mean, you can't ban all the naked ladies in the National Gallery, so I suppose Mizz Short thinks that the upper classes should be allowed to gaze at them in the National Gallery, but the workers shouldn't see them in the *Sun*. Unless she's against all paintings and statues like Cromwell, Michael Foot's favourite dictator.'

'You also talked about a return to Victorian values, but the greatest Victorians, like Dickens, spent their time denouncing the injustice of Victorian society and the evils of uninhibited capitalism.'

'That's right! It's exactly what the Earl of Shaftesbury did. He was a Conservative MP. You see, the Socialists talk a lot about compassion, but the Tories do something about it.' Mr Tebbit, having astutely snatched a Party political point out of the horrors of Victorian England, found his cheerfulness quite restored.

'You don't give any recreations in *Who's Who*. Is that because you haven't got any?'

'Really because I regard my private life as private. It has been rumoured that I do a little gardening.'

'What do you read?'

'Mainly those horrible red boxes!'

'Do you think you'll win the next election?'

'If we can desist from shooting ourselves in the foot. I'm opposed to us constantly doing that.'

'And what have you done with Jeffrey Archer?'

Although I had seen that ebullient author's name on a door on the way up I thought that since he told the young unemployed that he solved all his problems with a best-seller he had been kept bound and gagged in the cellar.

'Jeffrey's doing a terrific job speaking to the faithful.'

'But he's not allowed to speak to the world at large?'

'Oh yes he is. We had him on *Question Time*.'

'Who do you admire on the Labour benches? I imagine you might have a bit of a soft spot for Dennis Skinner.' It was an appealing thought, a glimmer of fellow feeling for the 'Beast of Bolsover' from the 'Hound of the Baskervilles'.

'Yes. Except when he goes right over the top. The world needs a Dennis Skinner. I don't think the world needs a Hattersley.'

'Anyone else?'

'Oh, I'd hate to ruin their careers by naming them.'

My three quarters of an hour had ticked away and Mr Tebbit was on his feet. I had time for one more question.

'If it became clear to you that by going on saying the things you've been saying you'd lose the next election, would you change them?'

'Of course not.' Mr Tebbit seemed only faintly amused by the suggestion. 'If the Conservatives wanted to change their policies they'd have to find another Chairman. I have to be true to what I stand for. And I shall go on expressing myself robustly.'

Although he has come in for more than his share of political abuse many people have experienced Mr Tebbit's considerable charm, and he is said to have earned the devotion of his Civil Servants, despite his habit of listening to Test Match commentaries during meetings. One MP called him a hard nut with a soft centre and even Mr Moss Evans, who Mr Tebbit would no doubt say is one of the 'cloth cap barons' of the trade union world, found him 'very scathing but without offence'. It seems clear that Mr Tebbit's particular brand of politics, by Friedrich von Hayek out of Edmonton County Grammar, is going out of style. Castigated by the electorate, the Conservative Party is now anxious to demonstrate its 'caring heart' and spend money, at least on education, which Mr Tebbit has called one of 'the soft issues'. He is probably too honest a man, and perhaps an insufficiently deft politician, to trim his sails to the prevailing wind. He may even feel, with one of his ironic little laughs, that he has, after all, nothing very much to lose. He is still playing with the casino's money.

FOR THE BEST IN PAPERBACKS, LOOK FOR THE

In every corner of the world, on every subject under the sun, Penguin represents quality and variety – the very best in publishing today.

For complete information about books available from Penguin – including Pelicans, Puffins, Peregrines and Penguin Classics – and how to order them, write to us at the appropriate address below. Please note that for copyright reasons the selection of books varies from country to country.

In the United Kingdom: For a complete list of books available from Penguin in the U.K., please write to *Dept E.P., Penguin Books Ltd, Harmondsworth, Middlesex, UB7 0DA*

In the United States: For a complete list of books available from Penguin in the U.S., please write to *Dept BA, Penguin, 299 Murray Hill Parkway, East Rutherford, New Jersey 07073*

In Canada: For a complete list of books available from Penguin in Canada, please write to *Penguin Books Canada Ltd, 2801 John Street, Markham, Ontario L3R 1B4*

In Australia: For a complete list of books available from Penguin in Australia, please write to the *Marketing Department, Penguin Books Australia Ltd, P.O. Box 257, Ringwood, Victoria 3134*

In New Zealand: For a complete list of books available from Penguin in New Zealand, please write to the *Marketing Department, Penguin Books (NZ) Ltd, Private Bag, Takapuna, Auckland 9*

In India: For a complete list of books available from Penguin, please write to *Penguin Overseas Ltd, 706 Eros Apartments, 56 Nehru Place, New Delhi, 110019*

In Holland: For a complete list of books available from Penguin in Holland, please write to *Penguin Books Nederland B.V., Postbus 195, NL–1380AD Weesp, Netherlands*

In Germany: For a complete list of books available from Penguin, please write to *Penguin Books Ltd, Friedrichstrasse 10 – 12, D–6000 Frankfurt Main 1, Federal Republic of Germany*

In Spain: For a complete list of books available from Penguin in Spain, please write to *Longman Penguin España, Calle San Nicolas 15, E–28013 Madrid, Spain*

A CHOICE OF PENGUINS

A Fortunate Grandchild 'Miss Read'

Grandma Read in Lewisham and Grandma Shafe in Walton on the Naze were totally different in appearance and outlook, but united in their affection for their grand-daughter – who grew up to become the much-loved and popular novelist.

The Ultimate Trivia Quiz Game Book Maureen and Alan Hiron

If you are immersed in trivia, addicted to quiz games, endlessly nosey, then this is the book for you: over 10,000 pieces of utterly dispensable information!

The Diary of Virginia Woolf
Five volumes, edited by Quentin Bell and Anne Olivier Bell

'As an account of the intellectual and cultural life of our century, Virginia Woolf's diaries are invaluable; as the record of one bruised and unquiet mind, they are unique' – Peter Ackroyd in the *Sunday Times*

Voices of the Old Sea Norman Lewis

'I will wager that *Voices of the Old Sea* will be a classic in the literature about Spain' – *Mail on Sunday*. 'Limpidly and lovingly Norman Lewis has caught the helpless, unwitting, often foolish, but always hopeful village in its dying summers, and saved the tragedy with sublime comedy' – *Observer*

The First World War A. J. P. Taylor

In this superb illustrated history, A. J. P. Taylor 'manages to say almost everything that is important for an understanding and, indeed, intellectual digestion of that vast event . . . A special text . . . a remarkable collection of photographs' – *Observer*

Ninety-Two Days Evelyn Waugh

With characteristic honesty, Evelyn Waugh here debunks the romantic notions attached to rough travelling: his journey in Guiana and Brazil is difficult, dangerous and extremely uncomfortable, and his account of it is witty and unquestionably compelling.

The Big Red Train Ride Eric Newby

From Moscow to the Pacific on the Trans-Siberian Railway is an eight-day journey of nearly six thousand miles through seven time zones. In 1977 Eric Newby set out with his wife, an official guide and a photographer on this journey. 'The best kind of travel book' – Paul Theroux

Star Wars Edited by E. P. Thompson

With contributions from Rip Bulkeley, John Pike, Ben Thompson and E. P. Thompson, and with a Foreward by Dorothy Hodgkin, OM, this is a major book which assesses all the arguments for Star Wars and proceeds to make a powerful – indeed unanswerable – case against it.

Selected Letters of Malcolm Lowry
Edited by Harvey Breit and Margerie Bonner Lowry

Lowry emerges from these letters not only as an extremely interesting man, but also a lovable one' – Philip Toynbee

PENGUIN CLASSICS OF WORLD ART

Each volume presents the complete paintings of the artist and includes: an introduction by a distinguished art historian, critical comments on the painter from his own time to the present day, 64 pages of full-colour plates, a chronological survey of his life and work, a basic bibliography, a fully illustrated and annotated *catalogue raisonné*.

Titles already published or in preparation

Botticelli, Bruegel, Canaletto, Caravaggio, Cézanne, Dürer, Giorgione, Giotto, Leonardo da Vinci, Manet, Mantegna, Michelangelo, Picasso, Piero della Francesca, Raphael, Rembrandt, Toulouse-Lautrec, van Eyck, Vermeer, Watteau

THE PENGUIN TRAVEL LIBRARY – A SELECTION

Hindoo Holiday   J. R. Ackerley
The Flight of Ikaros   Kevin Andrews
The Path to Rome   Hilaire Belloc
Looking for Dilmun   Geoffrey Bibby
First Russia, then Tibet   Robert Byron
Granite Island   Dorothy Carrington
The Worst Journey in the World   Apsley Cherry-Garrard
Hashish   Henry de Monfreid
Passages from Arabia Deserta   C. M. Doughty
Siren Land   Norman Douglas
Brazilian Adventure   Peter Fleming
The Hill of Devi   E. M. Forster
Journey to Kars   Philip Glazebrook
Pattern of Islands   Arthur Grimble
Writings from Japan   Lafcadio Hearn
A Little Tour in France   Henry James
Mornings in Mexico   D. H. Lawrence
Mani   Patrick Leigh Fermor
Stones of Florence and **Venice Observed**   Mary McCarthy
They went to Portugal   Rose Macaulay
Colossus of Maroussi   Henry Miller
Spain   Jan Morris
The Big Red Train Ride   Eric Newby
The Grand Irish Tour   Peter Somerville-Large
Marsh Arabs   Wilfred Thesiger
The Sea and The Jungle   H. M. Tomlinson
The House of Exile   Nora Wain
Ninety-Two Days   Evelyn Waugh

PENGUIN LITERARY BIOGRAPHIES

Sylvia Beach and the Lost Generation   Noel Riley Fitch
Arnold Bennett   Margaret Drabble
Elizabeth Bowen   Victoria Glendinning
Joseph Conrad   Jocelyn Baines
Scott Fitzgerald   André Le Vot
The Young Thomas Hardy   Robert Gittings
Ibsen   Michael Meyer
John Keats   Robert Gittings
Jack Kerouac: Memory Babe – A Critical Biography   Gerald Nicosia
Ezra Pound   Noel Stock
Dylan Thomas   Paul Ferris
Tolstoy   Henri Troyat
Evelyn Waugh   Christopher Sykes
Walt Whitman   Paul Zweig
Oscar Wilde   Hesketh Pearson

LIVES OF MODERN WOMEN

Titles already published, or in preparation

Hannah Arendt   Derwent May
Simone de Beauvoir   Lisa Appignanesi
Annie Besant   Rosemary Dinnage
Elizabeth Bowen   Patricia Craig
Vera Brittain   Hilary Bailey
Coco Chanel   Diane Johnson
Colette   Allan Massie
Margaret Mead   Phyllis Grosskurth
Christabel and Sylvia Pankhurst   Barbara Castle
Sylvia Plath   Anne Stevenson
Jean Rhys   Carole Angier
Bessie Smith   Elaine Feinstein
Freya Stark   Caroline Moorehead
Mme Sun Yat Sen   Jung Chang
Marina Tsetsayeva   Elaine Feinstein
Rebecca West   Fay Weldon

John Mortimer in Penguins

THE RUMPOLE BOOKS

'I thank heaven for small mercies. The first of these is
Rumpole' – Clive James in the *Observer*
'Rumpole must never retire' – Bill Grundy
'One of the great comic creations of modern times'
– Christopher Matthew in the *Standard*

THE FIRST RUMPOLE OMNIBUS

RUMPOLE AND THE GOLDEN THREAD

RUMPOLE FOR THE DEFENCE

RUMPOLE OF THE BAILEY

RUMPOLE'S RETURN

THE TRIALS OF RUMPOLE

RUMPOLE'S LAST CASE

PLAYS

A VOYAGE ROUND MY FATHER/THE DOCK BRIEF/
WHAT SHALL WE TELL CAROLINE?

EDWIN/BERMONDSEY/MARBLE ARCH/FEAR OF HEAVEN/
PRINCE OF DARKNESS

AUTOBIOGRAPHY

CLINGING TO THE WRECKAGE

'Enchantingly witty . . . should be held as the model for all
autobiographies of our times. England would be a poor place
without Mr Mortimer' – Auberon Waugh
'Exhilarating . . . hilarious . . . repays reading for its wisdom
and depth' – *Sunday Times*

PARADISE POSTPONED

'Hilarious and thoroughly recommended' – *Daily Telegraph*
'Hats off to John Mortimer. He's done it again' – *Spectator*

And

IN CHARACTER

THE PENGUIN LIVES AND LETTERS SERIES

A series of diaries and letters, journals and memoirs